VANESSA BOLOSIER is the founder of Carib Gourmet, which specializes in Caribbean food and confectionery, including the award-winning Coco Gourmand coconut sweets. She . also runs a cooking school and supper club in London. Half-Guadeloupian and half-Martiniquan, Vanessa was born and brought up in Guadeloupe and deeply immersed in the cooking of both islands. She moved to France at age 17 to work as a fashion model before moving to England.

Creole Kitchen

SUNSHINE FLAVORS
FROM THE CARIBBEAN

VANESSA BOLOSIER

weldon**owen**

TO PAPA, WHOSE HEART
AND SOUL WILL LIVE
FOREVER IN MY KITCHEN.

CONTENTS

INTRODUCTION: WELCOME TO MY CREOLE KITCHEN

In *Creole Kitchen*, you'll find sunshine and laughter, childhood memories, ancestral stories, and recipes that blend traditions and the culinary skills of everyone I've learned from throughout the years.

Over centuries, the Caribbean islands where I grew up—Guadeloupe and Martinique—have seen many changes and cultural influences; my food celebrates, honors, and remembers those influences, but also innovates, develops, and adapts. The food from my *Creole Kitchen* is a rich hybrid, resulting from the meeting of four continents. It reflects the Amerindians' love of seafood; the African tradition of using tubers in slow-cooked stews; French, Spanish, Portuguese, Dutch, and English cooking techniques applied to tropical ingredients; and Asia's myriad of spices used whenever possible. In my *Creole Kitchen*, you will encounter aromas you've never smelled before; for me, these smells remind me of home and trigger an instant sense of comfort.

I want this book to bring people together around the thing that matters the most when you celebrate life on the islands: food. It includes some treasured memories, such as the first time I was allowed to make a meat stew for Sunday lunch, thereby joining my family's "good cook club." It also looks at the traditions and festivals that give Creole cuisine its tempo. For instance, Christmas food was planned months ahead by fattening the pig for at least six months and drying orange peel to make the sacrosanct "shrubb" rum punch.

Most of all, the food and drinks from my *Creole Kitchen* are easy to make, easy to enjoy, easy to share. The recipes are based on classic dishes from Guadeloupe and Martinique; I have given them my personal touch, and you can adapt them to your taste. We are lucky to be living at a time when it is increasingly easy to find tropical vegetables and fruits in supermarkets and Asian and Afro-Caribbean shops and markets, but in some recipes, I have also suggested alternative ingredients to enable you to make them wherever you are.

I hope that these recipes will bring your friends and family together in the same way they have mine throughout the years. They will transport you to a tropical paradise and warm your heart and soul – or better still, inspire you to visit the islands of the French Caribbean. My *Creole Kitchen* is for the curious and the adventurous cook, with delicious recipes from my kitchen to yours.

MY CREOLE KITCHEN JOURNEY

THE GENESIS

Growing up in the Caribbean taught me about food: cooking seasonally, using locally grown fruits and vegetables, and identifying what's fresh and what isn't. I would often wake before dawn to go to the fish market with my dad to get freshly caught fish and seafood, still live and wriggling in the fishermen's boats. We also bought vegetables from the market ladies, who call you *doudou* (sweetheart) and always add a few limes or chiles to your bag when they've made a good sale. Avocados, papayas, guavas, carambolas, and many other exotic fruits grew in our garden, and we ate them on the spot, under the trees.

I'm a self-taught cook. My food mentor was my father. Men in the Caribbean don't tend to spend a lot of time in the kitchen – it's generally a female affair – but my father did. He was the eldest of several siblings, who were considerably younger than he was, and he learned to cook at an early age. His mother – who outlived him – is a market lady. As I write, she still sells anything from ginger shortbreads to vanilla pods, local fruits, and rum love potions in the Fort de France market in Martinique. My father spent the first few years of his life with his grandmother, an Amerindian who migrated from Dominica to Martinique. She taught him a few things about food but also how to smoke pure tobacco in a pipe, which he did all his life – almost like a ritual – after his Sunday nap. I would describe him as a bit of a feminist because of the very strong female role models he had growing up and his belief that women were indispensable, central, and crucial to any household, especially in the Caribbean because of the heritage from slavery. He knew that it wasn't just cooking and cleaning: they could do everything men could do – historically in the sugarcane and banana fields – and also had to carry and care for children in times when men were moved from one plantation to the other, leaving women to be the *poto mitan* (cornerstone) of the household. Memories of my father remain alive in my cooking. He was a very quiet man, and the kitchen was the place he opened up. We spent so much time together in the kitchen, and this is where he shared family secrets and funny stories, but above all, expressed himself.

I also learned, and still learn, a lot from my mother. Mamoune loves food and she has the sweetest tooth I know, which I have inherited. Caribbean food isn't generally known for desserts, but one of the many distinguishing features of Creole Caribbean food is its large variety of sweet things. Mamoune would make dessert on Sunday afternoons. She's a hands-on cook and always ends up taking the whisk out of my hands. She taught me to cook fast and efficiently; she also burns and cuts herself as much as I do. She was born in the town of Saint-Louis on the small island of Marie-Galante, an island I often revisit for its peace and quiet and its amazingly fresh Creole fish *court bouillon* (a tomato-based, very spicy broth in which parrotfish and many other colorful Caribbean fish are poached until tender).

A selection of family photos
from my childhood
in Guadeloupe.

▶

Dad chilling on the front terrace in 1998.

Me, my big sister, and my little brother.

I took this photo at my little cousin's birthday 14 years ago. He asked for a guava cake, and my mum ordered one just for him – he was so happy!

Dad and me before a Carnival dinner, hence the spotted bow tie (he was a pretty serious dude, so that's how far the costume went!).

Mum and Dad on their last cruise together in 2002. My mum is wearing a Creole *doudou* dress for the captain's dinner.

A formal portrait for my first communion with my mum, dad, sister, brother, and cousin Anthony.

I therefore grew up with an epicurean mother who enjoys fine foods and anything sweet and a father who loved the regional foods of his island and delighted in crafting authentic traditional slow-cooked stews. My approach to food definitely mingles the delicate and the rustic!

I grew up in Gosier, a rather touristic town in Grande-Terre in Guadeloupe. We lived on the inland side, surrounded by hills and greenery. My mother has a passion for gardening, and my father, who came from a very rural background, wanted the best of both worlds, proximity to the city and the ability to farm and live quietly. Our garden was naturally full of fruit trees of all sorts: three varieties of mangoes, oranges, limes, coconuts, Malay apples, ginep, guava, papaya, carambola, passion fruit, June plum, jimbilin, avocado, acerola, breadfruit – and I'm sure I've forgotten a few. I grew up with food on my doorstep. It's amazing how easy it is to fall in love with cooking when experimenting with ingredients only requires you to reach out and pick whatever is available. I have an older sister, but my brother is the one I shared my garden experiences with, eating fruits right under the trees and getting bellyaches because we ate too much, climbing trees, breaking trees, and getting told off because we broke the trees by climbing on them. We also went fishing – for rather questionable fish – in the nearby canals and helped our dad with the farm animals, running away from bees and other massive insects I still don't know the names of. My childhood was fun, filled with delight in the simple things.

When cooking, we experienced every single step of the process: getting itchy hands from peeling dasheen when its white sap touched our skin or stained black hands for days after peeling green bananas without first oiling our hands and killing animals, gutting and skinning them. We cooked in big pots, in fan ovens, on barbecues, on improvised *boucans* (charcoal grills), indoors, outdoors, on the beach, in the mountains. We cooked and ate everywhere, and that's the gel that keeps my family together: no matter what happens in our lives, when we cook together, all is well!

THE EXODUS

When I was 17 I moved to France, on my own, to study. I had obtained my baccalaureate a year early, and so I set out on my European adventures. Both of my parents had studied and worked in France and London when they were younger and had told us from an early age that after our baccalaureate, or when we turned 18, we should experience the rest of the world, study abroad, open our minds, and discover things. So I left my tiny island behind, not really knowing what to expect. I had travelled throughout my childhood, primarily in the Americas and the Caribbean, but I'd only been to France twice.

Cooking Creole food was a big challenge when I first arrived in France. My small studio and very limited access to ingredients were major deterrents, and when I was feeling nostalgic the only dish I cooked was *dombré et ouassous* (dumplings and prawns). When I moved to Paris and worked as a model while studying, I left Creole food aside because I rarely ate at home. I discovered some of the best foods in the world, ate at the most prestigious restaurants, but something was missing. My soul was starving. I longed for the aromas, the flavors, and the warmth I had experienced all my life. Every time I traveled home I would come back to France with suitcases full of foodie treasures. When my father passed away, I started cooking Creole food again, endlessly looking for the comfort I felt when cooking with him. It was my way of maintaining his legacy.

> "EATING CREOLE FOOD FEELS LIKE PRESSING PAUSE AND SOAKING IN THE WARMTH OF THE ISLANDS"

I moved to London in late 2005, and all of a sudden exotic ingredients were easily accessible. So I was able to re-create a truly authentic Creole kitchen, just like the one in which I grew up. Then I started cooking for my boyfriend. He's from West Africa and knew nothing about Caribbean food, but living with a Creole woman means you learn to love Creole food. I soon discovered the link between my food and that of Africa, as he marvelled at the many similarities.

I also cooked for other Creoles, from Haiti, Mauritius, and Réunion Island. We had long chats about the food with which we grew up and realized that although we were far from each other on the globe, we were so close in the kitchen. I cooked for my friends and colleagues, and I realized that they were all saying the same thing: eating Creole food feels like pressing pause and soaking in the warmth of the islands – escaping.

Coming to Europe and engaging with so many different cultures reinforced my culinary identity and also gave meaning to some aspects of my culinary culture I had never explored. I therefore decided to start cooking for others, people I didn't know. I organized supper clubs and cooking classes – a place where people yearning for soul food could come and recharge, but also could discover and experiment. My *Creole Kitchen* was born.

WHAT IS CREOLE?

When you say the word "Creole," many people automatically think of New Orleans, Louisiana. But Louisiana represents only a very small part of Creole culture. Creole was born of the convergence of people from many different horizons who needed to communicate. From that necessity arose a common language, albeit with a huge variety of dialects and accents, and a culture that embraces music and dance, art and architecture, folklore, myths, literature, games, rituals, festivals, and, above all, food.

The English word Creole, the French *créole*, Spanish *criollo*, and Portuguese *crioulo* all derive from the verb *criar* ("to breed") and the Latin *creare* ("to create"). It is associated with people who were born in a former colony, as opposed to those who migrated there as adults. My definition of Creole people with regard to the Caribbean – one that many people in the region will agree with – is that they are the descendants of slaves and laborers from different parts of Africa and Asia, living together on islands colonized by the French and English.

Creole people are mainly found in Haiti, Guadeloupe, Martinique, Dominica, French Guiana, and Saint Lucia, and also in Louisiana, Mauritius, the Seychelles, and Réunion Island. Other islands, such as Grenada, Saint Thomas, and Trinidad, have a residual Creole culture. Creole food is fascinating because of the many similarities in the cooking styles of people separated by thousands of miles across the globe.

MY CREOLE ROOTS

I'm a Creole from the French Caribbean, so most of my focus is on that region, specifically from Guadeloupe and Martinique, where my parents were born.

Guadeloupe and Martinique are overseas regions as well as *départements* of France, as are French Guiana in South America and Réunion in the Indian Ocean. All these places are French governed, with French as the official language; the inhabitants are born French nationals, they study the French curriculum in schools, and vote in all the French elections. They are part of the European Union – scattered pieces of France between the Atlantic and Caribbean Sea.

Guadeloupe
The island was named Karukera, "the island of beautiful waters," by its early inhabitants, the Caribs. It sits between Montserrat to the north and Dominica to the south. Guadeloupe is an archipelago covering about 600 square miles, composed of several islands, very different from one another. Mainland Guadeloupe comprises two islands, separated by a narrow strait: the rather flat Grande-Terre, with amazing sandy beaches, and hilly Basse-Terre, home to La Soufrière, an active sulphurous volcano. These two islands are shaped like a butterfly, which is why many Guadeloupians refer to their country as *"mon papillon."* There's also Marie-Galante, Désirade, and Les Saintes, which is actually two small islands, Terre de Haut and Terre de Bas. These smaller

islands offer a refuge when you want to soak up the real traditions of Guadeloupe and reminisce about the good old days. The total population of Guadeloupe is about 405,000 inhabitants.

Until recently the island of Saint Barths and half of Saint Martin were considered part of the archipelago of Guadeloupe, but since 2007 they have become more autonomous, although still French governed.

Martinique
The island was known to its original inhabitants as Madinina, "the island of flowers." Situated between Dominica and Saint Lucia, Martinique is a volcanic island of 400 square miles, with a population of approximately 390,000. Its famous volcano, Mont Pelée, erupted in 1902 and destroyed the entire town of Saint-Pierre, killing 30,000 people and leaving one survivor, a man who was in jail at the time. Today, Martinique is very Europeanized. It's modern, with a thriving tourist industry, an extensive road network, and great gastronomy, with prestigious chefs bringing contemporary French influences to Creole cuisine. The south is known for its sandy beaches, the north for volcanic sand and luscious forests. My father was from the town of Gros-Morne in the north, one of the most unspoiled places in the whole of Martinique.

▼ Map of the Lesser Antilles, showing Guadeloupe and Martinique.

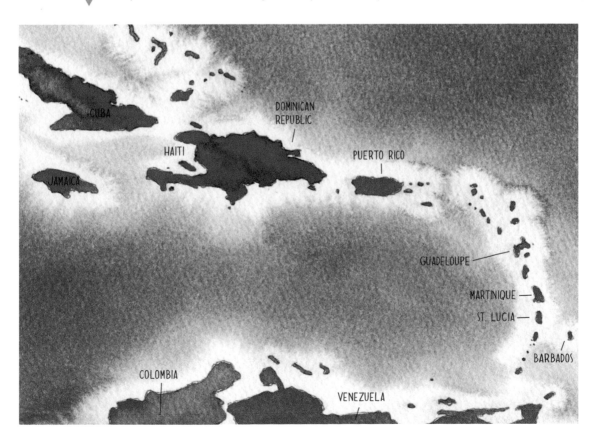

CREOLE FOOD: THE MELTING POT

Creole food is one of the first fusion foods, drawing influences from centuries of trading history and mixing cultures: it has been morphing, transforming, and evolving since the sixteenth century. It reflects the rich diversity of the environment in which it developed – the land, the ocean, the climate – and also the diversity of people on the islands. All these elements of place, culture, and ethnic mix created a vibrant cuisine. And although some might see the history of my island developing through slavery as a cause of sorrow, I embrace it and find in it tremendous wealth.

European colonization led to the creation of a society in which individuals and groups of people mixed. As the people mingled, they introduced their native, traditional, regional, or cultural identities to others and adopted new cooking techniques and ingredients. They created new dishes, developing them in a Caribbean context. Sharing is central to Creole culture, especially when it comes to food. Geography has also played a major part: proximity to South America and trade with Guiana and Venezuela introduced papaya, avocado, chocho (chayote), cocoa, and passion fruit to the Caribbean islands. The integration of these various elements created a distinctive cultural and culinary scene. While immigrants contributed traditional ingredients and dishes from their cultures, the combination of these ingredients and dishes creates a unique culinary fusion that is now recognized as Caribbean Creole cuisine.

It was not until I left Guadeloupe that I realized many Creole recipes that are fundamental to my culinary culture weren't quite as unique as I had imagined. I discovered that Colombo curry clearly originates in East India, the use of saltfish is a Portuguese tradition, and *doucelettes* are a coconut version of Scottish "tablet," a crumbly fudge. They are all found in the wonderful melting pot of Caribbean Creole.

I would have to say that my African ancestors have had the greatest impact on my personal identity. However, I can't ignore the influence my Amerindian great-grandmother had on my father, who passed on his knowledge of food and cooking to me. I also can't ignore my European roots – the story of my European ancestors is one of romance between a French pirate who decided to settle down with an Amerindian he met when he stopped off in Marie-Galante. Creole cuisine is full of stories of that sort, with the richness that comes from the intermingling of the islands' many settlers. It's fascinating to explore what was inherited from each wave of migration.

AMERINDIANS

The first settlers on the islands now known as the Petites Antilles (Lesser Antilles) were the Arawak, who arrived from South America in around 100 BC. After the ninth century, the Arawak were conquered by another South American people, the Kalinas or Kalinago, better known as the Caribs. The Amerindians were hunters, fishermen, and farmers.

The early food culture was based on what was available on each island. The Amerindians of the Lesser Antilles were known as "people of the sour cassava civilization." They practiced slash-and-

burn farming to clear land on which to grow cassava and maize. Cassava (also known as manioc or yucca) is a starchy tuberous root, which can be boiled and eaten as a vegetable or ground to make flour. The flour was primarily used to make a flatbread called *kassav*, cooked on a large round skillet heated over a wood fire, or *boucan*. With the juice of sour cassava, they made *ignari*, a sauce with hot chile peppers. They also made a fermented cassava drink called *ouicou*.

They lived near rivers and on the coast and used nets and harpoons to fish. Crabs, conch, prawns, crayfish, lobster, fish such as grouper, tuna, snapper, and shark, whale, dolphin, and tortoises were the staples of their diets. The indigenous Caribbeans also hunted various birds, rabbits, and other animals. In terms of cooking techniques, the Amerindians invented the barbecue: they grilled food on a framework of sticks, called *barbacoa*.

Native plants included diverse species of herbs, fruits, and vegetables, including *piments* (chile peppers), *ananas* (pineapple), *pomme cannelle* (sweetsop or sugar apple), *corossol* (soursop), guavas, and coconuts. Cassava (manioc), sweet potato, pumpkin, and certain types of peas and beans also grew wild on the islands.

When the newcomers settled on the islands, the Amerindians shared their knowledge about hundreds of plants used as medicines and as raw materials for tools – such as the *kwi*, a hollowed gourd used to carry water, and baskets – that are still made today following Amerindian tradition. My father often cured me and my siblings using the concoctions he learned to make from his Amerindian great-grandmother. He rarely used pharmacy medicine.

I have Carib ancestors on both sides of my family, something that's quite rare given that the Carib population was decimated by war and disease after the arrival of the colonizers. Many people from my islands view ourselves as heirs to the land through our Amerindian ancestry.

EUROPEANS

When Columbus came back to the Americas for the second time in 1493, the first island he set foot on was Kalouacera (or Karukera) – which means "the island of beautiful waters" – the name given by the Kalinago Amerindians to my native island, Guadeloupe. He disembarked in a cove near the present-day town of Sainte-Marie in Capesterre Belle-Eau. Columbus renamed the island "Santa Maria de Guadalupe," to fulfill a promise made during a pilgrimage in Spain at the convent of Santa Maria de Guadalupe de Extremadura. Explorers and colonizers renamed the islands and waterways, calling the region the West Indies because Columbus was hoping he was close to India and its abundance of spices.

For well over a century, the Spanish used the islands as a stopping point to get water before they set sail again, looking for gold in South America. They introduced some foods so they could replenish their ships' supplies, but didn't settle. The French and the English ended up battling it out for the islands of the Lesser Antilles for almost two hundred years, with the French finally gaining control of Guadeloupe in 1815.

The French and English conquests drastically affected every aspect of Caribbean life, and especially – both directly and indirectly – the cuisine. The colonizers introduced large-scale agricultural production on plantations, primarily a monoculture of sugarcane or banana, and eventually the islands supplied a large portion of the world's bananas, sugar, and rum, until South America took over in the nineteenth century. Nowadays sugarcane and its by-products are the second-largest export of the French Caribbean. Bananas are the first.

The Spanish introduced foods such as onions, garlic, cilantro, chickpeas, and oranges. Other Europeans, including the Portuguese, Dutch, Danish, British, French, and Swedish, came later to the islands, bringing their culinary trademarks such as the use of saltfish (from Portugal), pickling techniques, and various cakes and sweets. They also introduced foods from their trade with Asia, such as rice, limes, ginger, mangoes, and *malaka* (malacca apple, plum rose, or pomerac – a word derived from *pomme malaka*, French for Malaysian apple). Vanilla, native to Central America, was introduced to the Antilles by the French. Breadfruit was introduced from Tahiti in the late eighteenth century as a cheap source of high-energy food for slaves. The breeding of domesticated animals such as pigs, cows', and chickens replaced hunting as a source of meat.

Generally, the meals cooked for the colonizers were not eaten by anyone else. Most of the food we recognize as Creole is a legacy of the slaves and indentured servants. When it came to meat, the laborers were left with the parts of the animals that the Europeans didn't want. This is why pigs' tails, cow's feet, tripe, and other offal are frequently found in Creole single-pot stews.

However, a number of dishes brought during colonization were fully integrated into Creole cuisine: beef patties are a twist on British Cornish pasties; black pudding (*boudin noir*, blood sausage) was enjoyed in many parts of Europe, as were baked goods such as tarts, breads, and desserts such as rice puddings.

AFRICANS

The culinary traditions of Africa, as well as African flora and fauna, arrived in the Caribbean as an unintended consequence of the Atlantic slave trade.

The Caribbean was colonized by Europeans for the cultivation of commodities such as sugarcane and bananas. However, the locals did not take kindly to the idea of being reduced to slave labor on their own land. Around 60 years of conflict resulted in the partial extermination of the Amerindians, partly through fighting and partly because of alcohol and diseases they weren't exposed to before the arrival of the Europeans. The colonizers had to seek another labor force that could bear the hot, strenuous, and dangerous conditions presented by sugarcane or banana plantations: they found it in West Africa. The Portuguese were the first to engage in the transatlantic slave trade in the sixteenth century, and other countries soon followed.

Most African slaves were abducted to produce sugar, molasses, rum, and bananas, which have become very important foods in the Caribbean. I take pride in the fact that my African ancestors made these crops highly profitable, despite the very unfortunate conditions. If they hadn't been forced into labor, they would have enriched the African continent, it's true, but as a descendant, I can now take credit for the wealth of many western countries that were built on the profitability of this trade. I embrace the history that makes me who I am, and the slave trade was part of it.

In Africa, the diet would have included cassava and cornmeal, yams, dasheen (taro), peanuts (groundnuts/monkey nuts), watermelon, okra, pigeon peas, plantains, and bananas. These crops were transported to the New World along with the slaves – and their goats for milk and meat.

Although slow-cooked food is a direct heritage from the African continent, it was reinforced by the lifestyle of slaves on plantations. They worked long hours on the plantations, from very early morning to evening. They therefore had little time for preparing food and opted for slow-cooking stews that would simmer in one pot throughout the day while they worked. Slaves had very few possessions, so if they had a large pot, they had to make the most use of it. Another reason why slow-cooked stews are an important feature of Creole food is the fact that vegetables such as cassava and dasheen are toxic unless thoroughly cooked, while offal such as tails and feet needs a long cooking time to become tender.

If fish or vegetables were available, the slaves would use them in quick-fried foods such as fritters (*accras*) made with cornmeal. (Wheat flour entered the diet later and is what's mainly used nowadays for fritters and other fried foods.)

On some plantations, where slaves had their own huts, subsistence farming was common. The slaves grew their own food on plots near their huts, which allowed them to supplement their diets, grow plants from their native land, and cross native and foreign species. This reinforced the contribution of West African flora and cooking traditions to Caribbean Creole food culture. If they grew more than they needed, the slave women would sell it in the Sunday markets, a practice that exists to this day in Guadeloupe and Martinique – and pretty much throughout the Caribbean.

ASIANS

After slavery was abolished in 1848, plantation owners still needed low-cost labor to continue running their profitable trade. Immigrants from India arrived in the Caribbean through indentured servitude. They worked under contract to pay off their bill of passage. After they served their contracted years, they were free to either carry on working for the colonizers for low wages or go somewhere else. Many Indians decided to make a go of it on their own and built a small community of farmers. Their descendants still own melon, pineapple, and vegetable plantations, supplying local supermarkets and markets. They also farm the best goats to make Colombo curry, which is now considered to be one of the "national dishes" of the French Caribbean.

The Asian laborers brought their own culinary influences, with their use of spices, ingredients like mango and eggplant, and distinctive cooking styles and dishes. By adapting to the new environment, they soon became authentically Caribbean.

CREOLE CUISINE TODAY

Creole food is a vivid mosaic. For instance, the flagship dish in both Guadeloupe and Martinique is the Colombo curry, a true Creole production born of the contribution of the Asian settlers who brought spices, medicinal plants, and culinary secrets to the already vibrant cultural mix. On the islands you will find authentic Creole food in various forms: home cooking, street food, local restaurants, and gastronomic cuisine.

HOMEMADE FOOD

This is what you'll find in this book. It is about tradition (fish on Fridays, the all-day feast that is Sunday lunch, and Sunday night soup, or fat soup) and social expectations (the ritual of making *ti' punch*). There are distinctive regional dishes such as *bébélé* (a stew of tripe and a huge array of vegetables, with dumplings) from Marie-Galante, *pain au beurre et chocolat* (brioche with hot chocolate) from Martinique, and *tourment d'amour*, a cake from Les Saintes. Home cooking is often associated with religious celebrations and festivals; it's food that follows the calendar.

The first Sunday of January, Carnival kicks off. In Guadeloupe, and to a lesser extent in Martinique, every Sunday until Ash Wednesday is an opportunity to dress up and make Carnival fritters, such as banana fritters (p. 206) and eat street food like *bokits* (p. 100).

During Lent, meat consumption is restricted, but we eat fish cooked in many different ways.

Easter Sunday is lamb day; Easter Monday is crab day. Pentecost (fifty days after Easter Sunday) is another crab day.

Late spring and early summer is the season for weddings, christenings, first communions – and all sorts of other Catholic sacraments – inevitably followed by a party. Foods like *chaudeau* (a spiced milky hot drink) and *gâteau fouetté* (a light sponge cake covered with meringue) in Guadeloupe and *pain au beurre et chocolat* in Martinique are not to be missed!

Summer, which is all about grilled food on the beach, brings back some treasured memories of my childhood. Cycling is the most popular sport in Guadeloupe, so the Tour de la Guadeloupe in August is the event of the year. In Martinique, it's the traditional boat races during the Tour des Yoles Rondes. These events gave my family and me an opportunity to experience local specialities, as we visited every stop these tours made, whether in Martinique or Guadeloupe.

All Saints' Day, 1 November, when we honor the dead, is the time for soups. Families migrate to cemeteries, clean the tombs, light candles, and spend the night playing dominoes, drinking rum, and eating food alongside their deceased.

La fête des cuisinières is a yearly celebration of the best cooks in Guadeloupe, during which they parade in the streets in their best traditional attire.

▶

Throughout November and December, Chanté Nwèl is our extended celebration of Christmas, with local carols sung to the rhythm of drums and a feast of pork, with ham, pâtés, and ragouts.

STREET FOOD

In Guadeloupe and Martinique there are countless street vendors of all types of food. The influence of the original inhabitants of the islands, the Amerindians, is seen in the grilled meats and seafood such as conch and lobster. Grilled pork ribs are very popular, but the specialities are *poulet boucané* (buccaneer chicken) – charcoal-grilled chicken that's then smoked over sugarcane – and one of my favorites, *zail a dinde* or *ailes de dinde boucanées* – grilled turkey wings (p. 145) served with the unbeatable *sauce chien* (p. 190).

Bokits (p. 100) can be found all over Guadeloupe. They are fried dough sandwiches, like fried burgers, with various fillings, including saltfish, chicken, conch – the possibilities are endless. It's very similar to the Trinidad fried bake used for bake and shark, but strangely it is not found in Martinique or other Caribbean islands.

"Hot sandwich" is another popular street snack in Guadeloupe and Martinique. It's a type of thick baguette filled with anything from corned beef to liver or horsemeat.

The Creole islands are a melting pot of sweetness. "Cake ladies" are found at the markets, schools, churches, at small town fairs, and on the beach. They sell *tourment d'amour* (p. 208), pineapple upside-down cake (p. 220), coconut cake, marble cake, guava pastry (p. 226), and *jalousie banane* (p. 228), as well as traditional confectionery such as *tablette coco* (coconut drops), *doucelettes* (a crumbly coconut fudge), and *nougat pistache* (peanut brittle). They also sell what we call *sorbet*

au coco, (coconut sorbet), which is really coconut ice cream made in a rustic ice-cream maker. There's also refreshing *sinobol* (snowball), which is crushed ice covered with exotic syrups such as passion fruit and grenadine (p. 202).

LOCAL RESTAURANT FOOD

Small restaurants are where you eat at midday during your two-hour lunch break when you live in urban areas. In small towns they are the cornerstones of the community, restaurants passed down from generation to generation. They are often named after the grandmother who first owned them, or have simple names like *Le bord de mer* ("The seaside"), *Kaz a dodoze* ("Dodoze's house") or *An ba tol la* ("Under the tin roof"). The restaurants aren't fancy. They often feel like a small hut that could collapse at any moment. Extended families eat there, and you're welcomed the same way you would be if you went to your auntie's house, with a few pet names here and there.

The menu is much the same everywhere, Creole classics, similar to homemade food. You will almost certainly find saltfish fritters, *créole boudin*, and dressed crab, along with grilled or fried fish, the famous *court bouillon de poisson* (Caribbean Creole fish stew), king prawns either grilled or with *dombrés* (dumplings). You'll be offered grilled chicken, Colombo curry in many forms, octopus fricassée, sometimes conch fricassée, all of them served with red kidney bean consommé (beans stewed with vegetables and bacon), rice and beans, boiled vegetables, or gratins made with whatever they found at the market that day. Desserts are invariably coconut flan, flambé bananas, or scoops of mango, coconut, or vanilla ice cream.

The service is slow but that's a sign the food is freshly made, and there's always rum on the table to make *ti' punch* while you wait. These restaurants source amazing ingredients locally, and it's a unique opportunity to eat with the locals. The food is rustic; there's definitely no nonsense.

GASTRONOMIC FOOD

Guadeloupe and Martinique are overseas regions of France and are highly influenced by French culture. This means that there's a top-notch Creole gastronomic scene, with French-trained chefs taking Creole food to the next level. With recipes such as sea urchin flans, foie gras with plantains, duck breast with hibiscus coulis, scallops with orange-infused rum, lobster carpaccio, and banana crème brûlée, there's plenty to titillate your senses and to please the most refined palates.

This *doudou créole* has been working and smiling on the Marché aux Épices in Pointe à Pitre for the last 42 years.

WHAT'S IN MY CREOLE KITCHEN

There are a few basic utensils and ingredients you will need to re-create the atmosphere of a Creole kitchen and cook Creole food.

POTS AND UTENSILS

First among these is an old-school, very large, cast-iron pot with a tight-fitting lid, known in the United States as a Dutch oven. At least one. Creole food is family-style cooking, and you'll need room in your pot for all the ingredients. You could even invest in a vintage pot, because they say "the best soups are made in the oldest pots." A large, heavy-duty aluminium pot with a lid is an alternative found in many Caribbean kitchens. Lids are very important. I don't encourage you to cook Creole food in nonstick pans; sometimes you need the food to stick to create good flavors at the bottom of the pan, which you then deglaze with water, lime juice, or vinegar.

Other utensils are mostly things you may already have in your kitchen:
• large bowls for marinating
• some good sharp knives
• slotted spoons
• a wooden spatula or two
• a colander
• a sharp grater with large, medium, and small holes for grating coconuts, lime zest, and spices such as nutmeg and cinnamon
• a food processor to save hours of chopping and grinding
• a juicer to make coconut milk and pineapple juice

For Creole cooks, the *kwi* is a kitchen essential. It's half an emptied and dried calabash gourd used as a cup, bowl, scoop, or container for fresh spices, onions, garlic, limes, and chiles. My grandmother has one, my mother has one, and I have one. It's a thing you see in every Creole kitchen.

For making drinks and syrups, you will need some empty rum bottles (have a *ti' punch* party and keep the bottles) and a funnel. If you're using recently emptied rum bottles, there's no need to sterilize them – the lingering rum aromas will add a touch of extra character. Otherwise, you will need to sterilize them. Wash your bottles in hot water with antibacterial dish-washing liquid, place them in a preheated oven 225°F (110°C) for 15 minutes, and then remove them using oven mitts. You can use the same method for a metal funnel, but if you have a plastic funnel just wash it in hot water with antibacterial liquid.

INGREDIENTS

- Coconut vinegar—not essential, but we use it in many recipes in the same way as simple white vinegar, for example to deglaze a cooking pan
- Maggi (also known as KubOr) bouillon cubes – exported around the world for more than a hundred years, we often use these as a seasoning, crumbled into sauces and stews. You can get them online.
- Sunflower oil
- Vegetable oil
- White vinegar

Spices
- Allspice – a berry (known locally as *bois d'inde*) that combines the flavors of cloves, nutmeg, and cinnamon. We use it in many savory dishes, and it's easy to find ground allspice in shops and supermarkets.
- Black pepper
- Cinnamon – for a good fresh cinnamon flavor I use a cinnamon stick and grate it just before I need it. A pinch of cinnamon would be equal to giving the stick four strokes over the small holes of your grater.
- Cloves
- Colombo powder (p. 41)
- Fresh ginger
- Nutmeg – always use freshly grated nutmeg; a whole nutmeg will keep for ages in an airtight container. For a pinch of grated nutmeg, stroke it four times over the small holes of your grater.
- Pumpkin pie spice – this is the US equivalent of mixed spice, a blend of ground cinnamon, nutmeg, ginger, and cloves (sometimes including allspice) sold in the UK. I often use it with meat.
- Vanilla—preferably fresh vanilla pods; otherwise, use vanilla extract.

Herbs
- Bay leaves
- Fresh thyme – very important
- Garlic
- Parsley

Fruits and vegetables
- Avocados – large green ones
- Breadfruit – canned are fine when not in season
- Chiles – we use mainly hot varieties such as bird's-eye, habanero, and Scotch bonnet.
- Coconuts – some recipes call for grated fresh coconut meat, but unsweetened dried coconut can often be substituted; canned coconut milk is usually an acceptable substitute for fresh.
- Green onions (scallions) – we use both the white and the green parts.
- Mangoes
- Onions
- Pineapples – keep a few cans of pineapple slices in the cupboard.
- Tomatoes

Beans and peas (most types are available in both dried and canned forms)
- Brown lentils
- Green pigeon peas (gungo peas) – frozen, dried, or canned
- Mixed peas and beans
- Red kidney beans

THE THING WITH CREOLE CUISINE IS...

These are the ingredients, the techniques, and the elements you need to bear in mind before making Creole food. They are all important and will give you great insight into the culture.

INGREDIENTS

Piment (chile pepper)

Piman is the Creole word for chile pepper, and the chiles primarily used in Creole cooking are from the *Capsicum chinense* species, which includes some of the hottest varieties, such as habanero and Scotch bonnet. In the French Caribbean, the main chile we use is the habanero. We have two types: *bondamanjak* and *sept court bouillons*. In Creole, *bondamanjak* literally means "Madame Jacques' butt," and it got this name because of its shape, which resembles a large woman's butt. This is what I call red habanero chile. The sept court bouillons chile is known for being so strong that you could use the same chile to make seven successive court bouillons and it will be as hot and flavorsome in all seven of them. I call this Caribbean red habanero chile.

It can be tricky to find these chiles in some countries. Some people call all the yellow, orange, and red lantern-shaped hot chiles Scotch bonnet because of their fierce heat. But there is indeed a difference, which you can discover by experimenting with them, identifying the shapes, smelling them, and cooking with them. The most widely available hot chile in the UK is the Scotch bonnet – it's now sold in many supermarkets – and I have used it in many of the recipes in this book.

We also use a few other types of chiles, including the small green *piman-zozyo* (bird's-eye chile) and *piman-dou* (sweet chile pepper).

If you are really not keen on chile heat, there is another variety of *Capsicum chinense* called *aji dulce* (Spanish for sweet chile), or what in the French West Indies we call *piment végétarien*. It is related to the habanero and has similar aroma and flavor qualities to a good habanero pepper, but without the burn. They're not easy to find in shops and markets, but are quite easy to grow. They can be substituted for the hotter chiles in most recipes.

The majority of these recipes are not crafted to burn but to be flavorsome. Cooking the recipes with no chile at all will not achieve the same results. You can reduce the heat by removing the seeds and white membrane of the chile – where the substances responsible for burning are concentrated – and if you're really nervous, halve the amount of chile. My dad taught me that although we have to use it moderately, chile is known to reduce cholesterol and is great for your heart.

If you can't get enough chile, you'll find recipes for *piment confit* (chile pickle) and chile purée on p. 194.

Sugar

Creoles have a very sweet tooth, and since sugarcane products are a major export we are ambassadors for anything sweet. We traditionally use unrefined raw cane sugar and cane syrup, the special molasses-like syrup produced on the island of Marie-Galante, to make a wonderful array of confectionery and sugar-laden cakes; these items were an essential part of my childhood – no wonder I ended up creating my own confectionery brand. Many of my recipes call for raw or golden superfine sugar, which are less refined than the pure white sugars and retain some of the natural flavor of sugarcane. If you can't find golden superfine, you can substitute superfine (baker's sugar) or try whizzing raw sugar in the food processor. To make vanilla sugar, keep a scraped-out vanilla pod in a jar of superfine sugar.

Banana and plantain

Bananas are the major export of Guadeloupe and Martinique. We are proud of our bananas and there are adverts in both the French Caribbean and mainland France urging the French to consume only French bananas.

Creoles talk about "vegetable bananas" (green bananas) or "dessert bananas" (ripe bananas). They are part of many recipes and the vegetable bananas can be used as a substitute for ground provisions (hard food, see p. 40).

Green bananas are called *ti' nain* (small dwarf) in Martinique, *ti' fig* (small fig) in Guadeloupe. To prepare them, traditionally you'd begin by coating your hands with oil to prevent your hands from getting stained black; beware: the sap of the bananas can also stain your clothes. Traditional cooks first cut off both ends and then make a small slit lengthwise before peeling the bananas; they then scrape off the fibers that stick to the banana. I prefer to cut off the ends, cut the bananas in half, and then boil them with their skin on.

There are many varieties of dessert bananas. The *banane frécinette* is my favorite; it has a thin skin and is very sweet and fragrant. The *banane figue-pomme* is very fat and sweet, slightly bigger than the *frécinette*.

We call plantains "yellow bananas"; they are related to bananas but are always cooked, traditionally boiled in their skins. The unripe fruit is green and hard, ripening to yellow, then black. Depending on the recipe, they usually need to be pretty firm for savory dishes, but for sweet recipes they should be ripe and softer. Longer and thicker than bananas, you'll find them in Afro-Caribbean and Latin shops and markets.

Breadfruit

Breadfruit is controversial in the French Caribbean. Before Guadeloupe and Martinique became *départements* of France in 1946, the population consumed primarily locally sourced food; most of the food they ate was locally produced rather than imported. With the political transition, imports increased and new generations favored pasta over local vegetables such as breadfruit. Children started saying they hated it. Here's the issue: if the boats importing food were to stop coming, the locals would starve if they refused to eat locally produced food.

I'm "team breadfruit" and love it from starter to dessert. You can have it boiled, fried, or roasted with fish or meat, in fritters, soups, and stews. Breadfruit is good for you. It is high in dietary fiber and is a good source of vitamin C, and the starch and sugar make a very rich, energy-giving food. The milky juice it exudes can be applied to open wounds to help healing; the roots, when boiled, are a traditional medicine for asthma, skin diseases, and dental pain. An all-round superfood!

Cassava

The use of cassava (also known as manioc) in Creole food is a direct legacy of the original inhabitants of the islands, the Caribs. It is a large, long, tapered tuberous root with a thin, rough, dark brown skin and creamy-white flesh. Some varieties are classified as sour or bitter, others as "sweet"; both are poisonous when raw. Cassava can be boiled and served as a side dish or dried and ground to make flour. We use cassava flour in many recipes: to thicken stews and to make naturally gluten-free crepes, cookies, and a flatbread that we call *kassav*, traditionally filled with coconut jam, or more recently with savory delicacies such as conch or mackerel. Cassava flour is also used for its filling properties, especially in recipes like *féroce d'avocat* (p. 68).

The cassava flour we use in the Caribbean is not available in Europe, so in the recipes I've suggested you use *gari*, which you can find in Afro-Caribbean shops. Portuguese traders in the early sixteenth century took cassava from Brazil to West Africa, where it quickly became established as a staple food under the name *garri* or *gari*.

Coconut

When buying coconuts, you need to know what to look for. To ensure your coconut is fresh, shake the coconut close to your ear. If you hear the sound of water – not a sprinkle, a real wave of coconut water – it's good.

Coconuts have three eyes. One of them is the eye through which the coconut will germinate, which is slightly softer than the others; the only way to find it is to try all three. To drain the water from the coconut before you open it, pierce the softer eye using a nail or screwdriver and a hammer. I used to break my coconuts on the floor of my concrete yard in the Caribbean. Alternatively, break the husk with a hammer. Scoop out the flesh using an ordinary table knife or a spoon.

In the Caribbean we use grated fresh coconut, but unsweetened dried coconut is an acceptable substitute in many recipes.

To make coconut milk
You can make your own coconut milk by placing the fresh coconut flesh in a juicer, or blending it with 1⅔ cups (13 fl oz/400 ml) lukewarm water until completely puréed. You then strain the liquid through a kitchen towel or cheesecloth. Some supermarkets now sell chunks of fresh coconut, so you can make coconut milk without bashing a coconut husk. But if you're not feeling adventurous, canned coconut milk can be used in many of the recipes.

Giraumon

There isn't really a word to translate *giraumon*. It's a squash, a pumpkin, and it grows in the Caribbean and South America, where it's also called calabaza. In this book I use the term "calabaza" (West Indian pumpkin). In an Afro-Caribbean market, I just ask for pumpkin, they know what I mean. It's a weird-shaped pumpkin with green skin, often growing to an enormous size, and it is often sold already sliced. The flesh is sweet and slightly grainy. We eat it boiled, mashed in a dish called *giraumonade* (p. 171), in gratins, in soups, and in the stew we call *migan* (p. 133). It's used in Haitian Creole cuisine for the Independence Day soup they have on January 1. Some people still believe that applying a mash of *giraumon* to a boy's private parts will increase their size!

Lime

Lime is a key ingredient of many dishes and drinks in Creole food. Wedges of lime are often served with sliced chile for people to add their own seasoning to their food. We Creoles call it *citron vert*, (green lemon). The first time I cooked with yellow lemons was when I arrived in France. I looked for limes everywhere and when I couldn't find any, I ended up buying a yellow lemon, which I wasn't really sure of. When we were little, my mother would send us to collect limes from a tree. Markets sold only limes. I used limes in recipes and drank the juice of limes. That's why they are everywhere in my cooking.

When buying limes, they should be round, bright green, and feel heavy and juicy. Before cutting a lime, roll it firmly on your work surface to make sure you get all the juice you can out of it.

I also use lime juice to make a facial scrub. I got the recipe from my mum, who has one of the youngest-looking skins I've seen. Juice the flesh of 1 mango and mix with the juice of 1 lime and 3 tablespoons golden cane sugar.

Mango

I love mangoes, and in the Caribbean there are many varieties; we had *mangue-pomme* and *mangue-greffée* in our garden.

Apart from eating them fresh and using them in recipes such as mango gratin (p. 229), people use them in traditional medicine. Drinking water in which you have boiled mango seeds is said to cure diarrhea and worms. Mango leaf infusions can help cure rheumatism and are a diuretic. When cold pressed, the seeds produce a butter that can hydrate the driest hair and skin. Here's a recipe that I use on my very dry skin: juice the flesh of 1 – 2 mangoes and apply it to your hair, skin, face, or feet. Keep it on for 10 minutes, then rinse. Sounds messy? Just lie in the bathtub and let the mango work its magic.

Papaya

When you have one or two papaya trees in your garden, you know that when they're in season, you have more papayas than you could wish for. They very quickly go from green to ripe, so you are continuously cooking with them. I didn't like papayas until one day my dad candied them and flamed them with rum.

Papayas are very good for you, a great source of vitamin C and other nutrients, and my dad used to say that if I didn't want to lose my memory and wanted to keep focused, I should eat plenty of papayas. Not sure if that was just an attempt to make me eat them or whether it had any basis in fact. I know that on a recent visit home I had horrible joint pain due to a chikungunya mosquito bite; I drank an infusion of papaya leaves for two days and the pain disappeared.

Pineapple

As well as eating our very sweet pineapples freshly sliced, we include pineapples pretty much everywhere. Whether it's with pork for Christmas (p. 130), caramelized over upside-down cake (p. 220), macerated with wine and spices (p. 224), as jam or juice, I can say that pineapple is one of the top ten ingredients in our diet. Canned pineapple slices in juice (unsweetened) can be used instead of fresh.

There are many varieties of pineapples, but the one Guadeloupe and Martinique are best known for is the *bouteille*, a bottle-shaped pineapple with slightly less juicy but very sweet flesh. It's my favorite!

Sweet potato

The first time I saw an orange-fleshed sweet potato (what many Americans call a yam) was when I arrived in Europe. They weren't as sweet as the white-fleshed variety I had known all my life, but they look good on the plate. I now use three different types, and they are more or less interchangeable in recipes. I still prefer the white-fleshed ones, but they're not as readily available as their orange-fleshed counterparts. You can also buy purple-fleshed sweet potatoes, which look fabulous, especially when fried.

Calalou

Calalou (also spelled callaloo, with several variations) is found on every single Caribbean island. Although it is often said that the word is Portuguese, it actually comes from the Carib word *calao*, meaning a green stew. It travelled to Portugal with the early explorers and thence to Africa, and came back with the slaves and the leaves that today form the basis of the dish, dasheen (taro) leaves. Throughout most of the Caribbean calalou is made from almost any combination of crabmeat, fresh or dried fish, salt cod or stockfish, lamb, smoked meat, bacon or salt pork, garlic, okra, onions, tomatoes, spices, and, always, greens. However, in the Creole islands its main ingredient is crab. It's a slow-cooked stew with blue land crab, a slab of smoked bacon, pigs' tails, and dasheen leaves (spinach can be used as a substitute).

Crab

In Creole food we traditionally eat blue land crabs. They live in small holes in the ground near the sea, in mangrove swamps, and in humid valleys. They are usually caught in a very rustic trap. They can also be farmed and fed with chiles, herbs, spices, or fruits like mangoes. This will fatten them and flavor their flesh. However, they're not easy to find outside the Caribbean, so in my crab recipes you can substitute sea crab or crab claws.

Crab is big in Guadeloupe; there are even crab hunts when the hunting season is open. The small town of Morne à l'Eau in Guadeloupe holds an annual crab festival and has a crab museum that invented the crab rum punch.

But crab wasn't always so popular; it was once snubbed because of the lack of meat in its shells. In the eighteenth and nineteenth centuries, the Church imposed Lent on the slaves, and meat, even the offal, was forbidden. During that time, the slaves relied mainly on crabs as a source of protein. On Easter Sunday, they all came together in the black shack alleys to down the excess crab they had gathered. After abolition, crab was still viewed as slave food; the former slaves, when they could afford it, favored lamb and chicken for the Easter Sunday celebrations. Crab became Easter Monday food from 1884, the year Easter Monday became a public holiday.

I love crab, and we cook it in many different ways, the most widespread being the *matété* (p. 120) and *calalou*. Matété (*matoutou* in Martinique) is a Carib word, originally used for a large waterproof plate or table made of reeds and palm leaves. The dish that takes its name is similar to an American Creole jambalaya, but is made with crabs only.

Seafood

As well as crabs, other seafood is very popular throughout the Lesser Antilles. You could survive on these islands without ever eating meat – except for pork at Christmas – with seafood including octopus, conch, lobster, crayfish. My favorite is conch: it's not as available abroad, but if you can get your hands on some (try an Asian supermarket), it works well in a chicken stew similar to the octopus chicken (p. 142), grilled, or in a bokit.

Fish

Being islands, we are big on fish and very fussy. I had a hard time adapting to cold sea fish in my first few years in Europe. Although I now really enjoy seasonal local fish here, nothing replaces the colorful fish stalls you find in the ports of Guadeloupe and Martinique, the fish often still alive and jumping in the boat.

We rarely fillet fish. We use the whole fish: poached, stewed, grilled, or fried. Many food-lovers prefer the head of the fish to the rest of the body, and the head is where most of the health-promoting omega-3 fat is.

Parrotfish (which we call catfish) and *grand gueule* (the name means "big mouth" and locally we call it coney) are my favorite fish to make court bouillon with. The firmer-fleshed coney is added first and those with softer flesh such as the parrotfish go in later. To please everyone, my dad often

mixed fish. There was always a snapper somewhere in the mix: glass-eye snapper, yellowtail snapper, or red snapper. We use dorado (sometimes known as mahi-mahi), certain types of sea bass and groupers, shark, red mullet, golden mullet, red butterfish, and pink sea bream. Each fish has its own characteristics, and there's no substitute, but if you really cannot get your hands on any of these, a good firm-fleshed whitefish will do, and I have suggested alternatives in some recipes.

Nowadays in the islands' fish markets, fishermen will have someone clean your fish. This wasn't always the case, and as children it was our duty to gut and clean them. This was the best way to understand each fish and enjoy cooking it. Most fishmongers today will clean fish for you but it's good to check the fish before starting to cook. First, I check my fish for any trace of scales. Nine times out of ten the gills won't have been removed so I take them out by pulling them downwards. I clean inside the fish, taking care to scrape out any blood clots, which would ruin the taste of your dish. I rub half a lime inside the fish – partly for flavor, partly because that's what I was taught to do – and if marinating, I suggest turning the lime upside down and leaving it inside the fish until ready to cook. Don't forget to remove it before cooking.

Saltfish and smoked herring

Saltfish – generally understood to mean dried salted cod – is a Caribbean classic, cooked in a myriad of ways. It was introduced by the early European explorers, who needed a source of food that would not spoil during their long sea voyages, and in the hot Caribbean climate it has proved to be an invaluable pantry item. Smoking is another way of drying fish to preserve them, and smoked herring are at the heart of many Creole dishes.

Many supermarkets sell boneless, skinless dried salted cod in their world food sections. Unless otherwise specified in the recipe, always go for this type: it will make your life easier. Before using it, you will need to desalt it. The quickest way is to put it in a pan with cold water, bring it to a boil, and boil for 5 minutes; you then drain off the water and repeat the process.

The Europeans also preserved herring by smoking, which allowed them to be kept for many months, and smoked herring (similar to English kippers) remain popular in the French Caribbean. We desalt them by boiling them for 5 minutes before using them.

Pork

Pork is far and away the most important meat in Creole cuisine. Pigs arrived in the Caribbean with the European colonizers. At first they brought salt pork, smoked bacon, and hams that had been cured to keep during the Atlantic crossing, but they soon introduced domesticated pigs to be farmed, and pork entered the Creole diet. During the centuries of slavery, most Creoles had access only to the unwanted parts of the pig, but nowadays the whole animal is used. There's a tradition of adding pork meat to a meal to add flavor, and that's why you'll find it in so many recipes, even in seafood dishes.

The centerpiece of the Christmas feast is Creole pork ragout (p. 130), and I remember hearing the pigs squealing in the distance the day before Christmas Eve – they knew their time was up! One year we had a pig named Priscilla. My brother and I were in charge of feeding her, until she got too big and my dad concluded it was time to eat her before she ate us. My dad insisted we learn to farm and kill our animals in order to understand how every stage of the process was important in order to produce good meat. I was used to raising – and killing – animals, which taught me everything I need to know about meat. We had rabbits, chickens, geese, quails, and pigeons – but pork is still my favorite meat.

Offal

Creoles believe in nose-to-tail eating, and if you only remember one Creole expression from this book it should be *ayin pa ka pèd* – "nothing is wasted." It's a mentality that stems from slavery and a time when unwanted things, including food, could be someone else's treasures. My ancestors survived on offal such as pigs' tails and trotters, cows' feet, tripe, and hearts, and although it's no longer necessary for Creoles to eat them, they are integral to our cuisine.

Offal must be very fresh – especially kidneys, which will quickly taint and become bitter. It should look glistening (not slimy) and firm. Avoid dry, cracked, or bad-smelling offal. Some people are put off by the strong smells and flavors of offal such as kidneys and liver; for a milder-tasting offal, try heart, sweetbreads, or tripe.

It isn't always easy to find trotters, snouts, and tails (which are sold salted and cured). Make friends with your butcher and you'll secure fresh offal. Exotic markets and butchers serving an ethnic community often have various items, although you may need to order in advance. Some online retailers also sell salted pigs' tails and other items.

When using offal in Creole cooking, it is imperative to prepare it the following way:
1. Clean thoroughly in cold water. **2**. Remove any blood vessels and sinews. **3**. Soak overnight in lime juice and water. **4**. Boil with bay leaves and salt (unless desalting pigs' tails and snout). **5**. Clean under fresh water. **6**. Cut into small chunks.

Outside the Caribbean, tripe is often sold precooked and cleaned and does not need the long, slow cooking required in many Caribbean recipes. Ask your butcher for advice.

Preserved food

Creole food includes a lot of preserved meat and fish, and Creoles *love* anything cured, smoked, or salted. This dates back hundreds of years, to when the European colonizers introduced their traditions of processing meat and fish in various ways so they would keep during the crossing of the Atlantic. As well as salted and smoked fish, we use salted beef, similar to corned beef, and smoked bacon, the latter cut in thick lardons from a slab. Ask your butcher or look online.

Canned food

In Creole food, we don't snub cans. There's actually a tradition of consuming certain processed foods, such as corned beef (canned pressed beef), sardines, condensed and evaporated milk, and even canned salted butter. This is especially true during the hurricane season (July to November). When the hurricane season starts, families stock up on canned food, cured meats and fish, and dry goods like flour. These will help them survive in case of water cuts, electricity cuts, and being unable to get to the shops for days or weeks.

TECHNIQUES

Cleaning

The tradition of cleaning fresh meat and fish with lime juice goes back to the context in which Creole food was born. The Creole islands are obviously in a hot climate. Until the mid-1950s, electricity was rare. Things were either consumed very fresh or were preserved in some way – canned, cured, salted, dried, or preserved in vinegar or sugar. With no refrigerator to keep produce fresh you *had* to clean your meat and fish to kill all bacteria; this is why we rub raw fish, poultry, and meat with lime juice.

I still clean fresh meat and fish in this way because it has an impact on the taste of the food and because I grew up doing it. In cooler climates it is not strictly necessary, but now you know why we do it in Creole cooking.

When It comes to fruits, they are also often washed and cleaned with lime juice before any further preparation. Fruits from your own garden or from local markets (from small cash-crop farmers) might have been visited by little insects or other creatures; the lime juice scares them off! Otherwise, a simple wash under fresh water is fine.

Seasoning

The Creole term *assaisonnement* describes the principal of marinating fish, poultry, and meat. This "seasoning" is always based around the same ingredients: thyme, hot chile pepper, lime, and garlic. Traditionally, whenever you use meat or fish – unless it's offal, which requires another approach (p. 37) – you have to marinate it, preferably the night before but at least 2 hours before cooking.

First check your meat or fish for freshness, then remove excess fat, hair, or scales, and blood clots. Forgetting these small steps can ruin your dish. Put the fish or meat in a bowl, add the thyme, chile, lime, and garlic, plus a splash of water for fish or oil for meat. You can add bay leaves if you wish. For meat I also like to add a pinch of ground allspice and a pinch of mixed (pumpkin pie) spice; it seems to make the meat more tender and adds great flavor.

Chopping finely (mincing)

You will see the instruction "chop very finely" throughout the book. This was my nemesis when learning to cook with my dad. Nothing was ever chopped finely enough. The tradition of chopping things finely comes from the need of post-slavery field workers to cook food quickly; when mothers came home from working in the field, they had to feed their children. It also saved fuel and made things easy to eat with the fingers: until the twentieth century, cutlery was a luxury for the workers.

Deep-frying

Power cuts are common during the hurricane season, and most people keep a disposable gas burner in their kitchen. That's when a lot of deep-frying is done: bokits and fritters are the mainstay of the diet during that time.

KEY ELEMENTS OF CREOLE FOOD

Accras

Accras are small fritters, and in the Caribbean they are eaten almost every day in one form or another. The name comes from the word *akara*, which in Wolof, a Senegalese language, means "black-eyed pea beignets." A similar word in Ewe, another West African language, means "vegetable beignets."

Originally made with vegetables, accras are now widespread, and the range of things you can put in the dough has been extended to include salt cod, smoked herring, crab, conch, octopus, shrimp, and lobster. On Good Friday, the majority of the islanders, being practicing Christians, have malanga (eddo), *giraumon*, carrot, or cabbage accras as part of the meatless fast for the occasion.

Ground provisions (hard food)

Creoles say *racines*, which means roots (tubers): yam (true yam, not to be confused with the orange-fleshed sweet potatoes often called yams in the US), sweet potato, dasheen (taro), and malanga (eddo). They are usually just boiled with salt and served with fish and meat; this is what you expect as a side dish. The term has now been extended to include green bananas, plantains, breadfruit, and chocho (chayote).

Bokits

The bokit, rather like a deep-fried burger, dates back to the mid-nineteenth century, after the abolition of slavery. The workers were so poor they couldn't afford real bread from the baker, but instead made a basic dough and fried it in a pan full of hot oil.

According to Jacques Dancale – who wrote a whole book about bokits, *Voyage au pays du bokit* (2004) – they were brought to the Caribbean by New England colonizers who copied a recipe from the Shawnees, a native North American tribe, for corn cakes called *jonikin*. The colonizers added wheat flour and called it "journey cake" since it could last many weeks at sea. In the end, the name "johnny cake" stuck and versions are found across the Caribbean. When it reached the French islands, they heard "*djonkit*" or "*dankit*" (that's what my grandparents called it). Over time it changed shape and content, and in Guadeloupe it ended up as bokit. I've included a recipe for my favorite bokit (corned beef bokit, p. 100).

Funnily enough, bokit doesn't exist in Martinique. However, bokit is very similar to bake and shark, a Trinidad classic, and I guess it probably has the same origins.

Colombo powder

Many of the Indian migrants who arrived around 1862, bringing with them their traditional spice mixes, came from southern India and Ceylon (now Sri Lanka), whose capital city is Colombo. That's where the flagship dish of Martinique and Guadeloupe gets its name. It's a curry that we make with mutton, pork, chicken, fish, and shrimp, flavored with the following blend of spices.

2 tbsp coriander seeds
2 tbsp ground turmeric
1 tbsp cumin seeds
1 tbsp mustard seeds
½ tbsp fenugreek seeds
1 clove
1 tbsp garlic powder

Put all the spices in a spice grinder or mortar and pestle and grind to a powder. Pour it through a fine sieve and keep it in an airtight container. Try to use it fresh or within 2 – 3 months.

Dombrés

Dombrés – believe it or not – got their name from English. When the English occupied the French islands in the eighteenth century, they kept their prisoners, known as "the damned," in the caves below their forts. The bread they threw at the prisoners was a very basic bread made of water, flour, and salt; it started off being called "damned bread," and soon became *dombrés*.

After a while, the name dombrés came to be used for small balls of a basic flour and water dough, similar to dumplings. Added to stews made with red kidney beans and pigs' tails, crab, shrimp, or crayfish, they provided energy for the field workers. Despite their poverty, the slaves and laborers showed great ingenuity in making their dishes interesting and tasty. If they worked near a river or the sea, they were able to catch crayfish, large prawns, or land crabs – and any other shellfish they could get their hands on; it all went into the pot with the dombrés.

This is how you make dombrés:
3¾ cups (14 oz/440 g) all-purpose flour
1 cup (8 fl oz/250 ml) cold water
1 tsp salt

Put the flour in a large mixing bowl and make a well in the center. Add the water and salt to the well. Mix and knead until you have a ball of dough that does not stick to your fingers.

Pinch off a piece of dough about ¾ inch (2 cm) in diameter and roll it into a small ball. Continue making small balls until you've used up all the dough.

Dombrés will cook through in the sauce of a recipe, usually for about 20–30 minutes; follow individual recipe instructions.

Rhum agricole

Sugarcane is important in the French West Indies. We chew the sugarcane, we drink the juice. But its most popular form is rum. Rum played a large part in the Creole lifestyle until relatively recently. The workers who planted and cut the cane in the fields may have started their day at 5 a.m. with a *décollage* (take-off). Around 9 a.m. it was time for the *sec* (dry), which is rum with lime zest and a few grains of brown sugar. Midday was time for *ti' punch* (it means "small punch," but it is the national drink of Guadeloupe and Martinique, a combination of rum, lime juice, and sugar). Religion was not forgotten: 3 p.m. marked *l'heure du Christ* (hour of Christ) and 5 p.m. *ti' pape* (small pope). After finishing work they had a *pété-pié*, which means "it breaks your feet," and by now you might expect them to be falling over. Yet some men still had the capacity for a "CRS" (*citron*, *rhum*, *sucre* or lime, rum, sugar).

Rhum agricole – produced from sugarcane juice as opposed to molasses (a by-product of sugar refining) – is pretty special, and most people from Guadeloupe, Martinique, and Haiti are bound to be rum snobs. Growing up in a nation where *rhum agricole* is produced shapes your views (and taste buds) when it comes to rum. I have my own little rum cave full of anything from 100-year-old *rhum agricole* to white rums that I use almost every day.

I don't advise using *rhum agricole* in everything because it is very expensive, especially the aged rums from Martinique and Guadeloupe. But I do recommend keeping at least one good bottle of white *rhum agricole* to make the cocktails in this book. If you can't get your hands on Guadeloupe or Martinique *rhum agricole*, you could use a Barbancourt from Haiti. If you still struggle, use a 6- to 12-year-old rum from any well-known brand.

Music

We have fun in the kitchen. Kassav, the band that invented *zouk* (a musical style originating in Guadeloupe and Martinique), and Tabou Combo, the grandfathers of *compas* (from Haiti), were the soundtracks to cooking throughout my childhood. We'd put on the radio and sing along. Want to be in the mood for some Creole cooking? Put the music on!

BWOISSON

DRINKS

◆◆◆◆◆◆◆◆◆◆

Guadeloupe and Martinique are among the most prolific
rum-producing islands, producing some of the world's
best rum — *rhum agricole* — which is distilled from fresh
sugarcane juice rather than molasses. On Sundays my dad
would take the whole family on long drives to discover
the island, and he often told us stories about the illustrious
past of Guadeloupe in the sugar and rum trade. As I write
this, I can recall the smell of molasses from the factories
we drove past and visited.

I love all rums, but I wouldn't have my cocktails made with
anything other than *rhum agricole*, since, just like Obélix, I fell
into this magic potion at an early age. However, there are some
very good industrial rums that can replace *rhum agricole*; the
cocktail will not taste quite the same but will still be delicious.

Some of these drinks need to macerate or mature for a few
weeks or months. You'll need some sterilized glass jars or empty
rum bottles and a funnel to pour the liquid into the containers.

COCONUT PUNCH

Having *punch coco* for Christmas in the Caribbean Creole islands is a tradition, like having eggnog in the US or mulled wine in the UK. From the time I was eight years old and my brother was five, we were allowed a finger of coconut punch every Christmas, which we loved not for the rum, but for its deliciously creamy taste.

Serves 8–10

⅞ cup (7 fl oz/200 ml) white
   rhum agricole
1⅔ cups (13 fl oz/400 ml) coconut
   milk
⅞ cup (7 fl oz/200 ml) condensed
   milk
⅔ cup (5 fl oz/150 ml) cane syrup
   (p. 198)
2 pinches grated cinnamon
1 pinch grated nutmeg
grated zest of 1 lime
1 vanilla pod, cut in half
   lengthwise

Put the rum, coconut milk, condensed milk, and cane syrup in a large mixing bowl. Stir with a wooden spoon until rich and thick.

Add the cinnamon, nutmeg, and lime zest. Using a small knife, scrape the seeds from the vanilla pod and add to the bowl. Stir until evenly mixed.

Using a funnel, pour the coconut punch into an empty rum bottle (sterilized if necessary, see p. 24) and place in the refrigerator for at least 2 hours. You can keep it in the refrigerator for up to 2 months.

Shake well before serving.

TIP

This is best made with freshly grated cinnamon stick and whole nutmeg and a fresh vanilla pod. However, you can use ground cinnamon and nutmeg and replace the vanilla pod with 1 tablespoon vanilla extract.

COOLLY

I have always loved lychees. This fruit is very rare in Guadeloupe and mainly grows on the leeward coast. If you're lucky enough to know someone who has a tree to give you a box or two every season, you make the most of it.

Serves 4

2 cups (16 fl oz/500 ml) cane syrup
  (p. 198)
juice of 8 limes
½ cup (4 fl oz/125 ml) white
  rhum agricole
½ cup (4 fl oz/125 ml) coconut water
4–8 lychees, peeled and deseeded, or
  use canned lychees if not in season

Pour the cane syrup into a jug. Add the lime juice, rum, and coconut water and stir until thoroughly mixed. Place in the refrigerator for at least 3–4 hours.

Put some crushed ice into each glass and add one or two lychees, then pour in the cocktail.

BAVAROISE À LA PAPAYE

PAPACOCO

When you have papaya trees, you know they can be very prolific. In the Caribbean, a *bavaroise* has come to mean a milky (and often alcoholic) fruit drink – quite different from the creamy, fruity French dessert *bavarois* that is set with gelatin. The most popular *bavaroises* are soursop, papaya, and guava. When my dad used to make this milky drink with papaya juice after our morning run on Sundays, I knew we were in for a treat even though papaya wasn't my favorite thing. He made it with condensed milk, but here I've used rum and coconut milk and made it an adult drink.

Serves 4

2 large ripe papayas, peeled, halved, and seeds scooped out
2½ cups (20 fl oz/600 ml) coconut milk
1⅔ cups (13 fl oz/400 ml) white rhum agricole
1 pinch grated cinnamon
1 tsp vanilla extract

Blend the papaya flesh with the coconut milk, then pass through a fine sieve into a bowl.

Add the rum, cinnamon, and vanilla and stir.

Transfer to a cocktail shaker and shake well or pour into a large jug and whisk vigorously. Put some ice cubes into each glass and pour in the cocktail. Drink immediately, before the papaya starts to separate from the milk.

SHRUBB

Shrubb is a very traditional Christmas liqueur — the drink my dad loved to make above all others. My father's childhood wasn't the best — he grew up very poor, and Christmas held a very precious place in his heart because it was the only time of year he was really allowed to be a child, have fun, and indulge. Dad would have stars in his eyes when talking about this drink, and from October we would eat mountains of oranges so he could dry the peel to make shrubb. He made several types: strong shrubbs, sweeter ones, a mild version for the children, and flavored shrubbs with star anise in some, cardamom in others, or a mix of orange and clementine. His shrubbs infused for a good 40 days to be perfect and ready to be downed during Christmas celebrations.

**Makes about 5 cups
   (40 fl oz/1.2 liters)**

3 oranges
1 bottle (750 ml) white rhum agricole
2 cups (16 fl oz/500 ml) cane syrup
   (p. 198)
1 cinnamon stick
1 pinch grated nutmeg
1 star anise
1 vanilla pod, cut in half lengthwise

Peel the oranges in long strips, removing only the zest and ensuring that none of the bitter white pith is left on. Leave the zest to dry for at least a week, preferably in direct sunlight.

Once dry, place the orange zest in the bottle of rum and leave to infuse for a week.

Pour the rum and orange zest into a sterilized 1½-quart (1.5-liter) preserving jar. Add the syrup, cinnamon, nutmeg, star anise, and vanilla pod and mix well. Leave to infuse for 3 weeks.

Strain the rum through a fine sieve into a large jug, discard the zest and spices, and pour back into the empty rum bottle, using a funnel. It will keep in a dark cupboard for 6 months.

Serve with an ice cube.

TIP

Back home we buy rum in
1.5-liter bottles, an empty
one of which would be ideal
for infusing this shrubb.
If you haven't got one of these,
use two smaller bottles
or a 1½-quart (1.5-liter)
preserving jar.

TI' PUNCH

Ti' punch is simply a Creole institution, a real representation of the culture of Guadeloupe and Martinique. Ti' punch is a very easy-to-make short cocktail. Tradition demands that ti' punch not be prepared in advance: instead, the ingredients are left on the table for guests to make up their own. Almost like a ritual, you have to take your time, sip, and savor.

This cocktail can be made only with *rhum agricole;* it can be white or aged, but don't you dare try to make a ti' punch with anything else. It would be a sin, just as adding an ice cube would be considered a real insult to the purists. Don't underestimate this little punch. Drink it moderately.

This is the basic recipe for one person, but make it your own—that's what ti' punch is all about.

Serves 1

½ lime
2 tsp golden superfine sugar
    or light soft brown sugar
    (or 1 tsp cane syrup, p. 198)
generous 3 tbsp (1½ fl oz/50 ml)
    white rhum agricole

Squeeze the lime into a small glass (keep the squeezed lime) and add the sugar.

Stir with a teaspoon (or, if you have one, a *bwa lélé*, a small stick with branches at the end, used as a whisk) until the sugar has dissolved.

Put the squeezed lime in the glass. Pour in the rum (no ice). Enjoy!

SORREL (HIBISCUS) DRINK

When people are enjoying their rum-laced sorrel punch during the extended Christmas celebrations called *Chanté Nwèl*, this sorrel drink is the nonalcoholic alternative. It's a festive, spicy drink, evocative of my childhood singing carols in Creole throughout Advent and Christmas.

Serves 4

4 oz (100 g) dried sorrel (hibiscus)
    petals
1 cinnamon stick
1 quart (32 fl oz/1 liter) water
2 tbsp raw sugar
1 tbsp vanilla sugar (p. 28)
 a few mint leaves (optional)

Put the sorrel, cinnamon, and water in a saucepan. Bring to a boil and boil for 15 minutes, then leave to cool.

Scoop out the petals. Add the cane sugar and vanilla sugar and stir well until the sugar has dissolved. Place in the refrigerator for at least 3 hours.

Serve with ice, and a few mint leaves, if you like.

TIP

In the Caribbean, sorrel means the red flower of the hibiscus. We use it to make drinks (both alcoholic and nonalcoholic) and in cakes. You may be more familiar with it than you think: it's used in herbal teas for its color and flavor. You can buy dried hibiscus flowers in Afro-Caribbean, Latin, Turkish, and Persian shops.

JUS DE GINGEMBRE / GNAMAKOUDJI

GINGER JUICE

This recipe isn't technically completely Creole. My West African boyfriend craved his favorite childhood drink, and so his mother taught me how to make this juice. One day during a trip back home, I served it to my mother and cousins. They argued that this drink was the soft version of a well-known love cocktail reputed to ignite amorous flames, which includes a so-called aphrodisiac bark we call *bois bandé*. Not sure how true that is, but this juice will definitely give you a kick when needed.

Serves 4

6-inch (15-cm) piece fresh ginger, peeled
10 oz (300 g) fresh pineapple, peeled, or 10 oz (300 g) drained canned unsweetened pineapple slices or chunks
juice of 3 limes
1 quart (32 fl oz/1 liter) water
1½ cups (12 oz/300 g) raw sugar

Process the ginger and pineapple in a juicer. Transfer to a bowl or large jug, add the lime juice, and stir, then add the water and stir well until thoroughly mixed. Alternatively, if you don't have a juicer, use a blender to purée the ginger and pineapple with the lime juice and water and then pour through a fine sieve.

Add the sugar to the juice and stir well until the sugar has dissolved. Place in the refrigerator for at least 3 hours.

Serve with ice cubes.

To transform this cocktail into a love potion, add some rum and grated cinnamon.

PUNCH ANANAS

PINEAPPLE PUNCH

When it's pineapple season in Guadeloupe, the fruits are thrown at you left, right, and center, and you find yourself including them in pretty much everything.

Serves 8–10

2 very sweet ripe pineapples, peeled, cored and cut into chunks, or two 14-oz (400-g) cans unsweetened pineapple slices or chunks
½ cup (4 oz/100 g) raw sugar
1 tsp vanilla extract
2 cups (16 fl oz/500 ml) white rhum agricole

Purée the pineapple in a food processor. Tip the pineapple purée into a large bowl and add the sugar and vanilla. Stir and cover with plastic wrap. Place in the refrigerator for 24 hours.

Pour the pineapple into a saucepan and cook over low heat for 20 minutes. Leave to cool.

Add the rum and stir, then put the mixture back in the refrigerator for 4 hours. Serve well chilled.

PUNCH BANANE

BANANA PUNCH

Bananas are the main export of Guadeloupe and Martinique and are very important in Creole gastronomy. This punch is a tribute to my islands' precious commodity. It's creamy and sweet and must be drunk on the day that you make it—it won't keep.

Serves 4

4 bananas
juice of 3 limes
½ cup (4 fl oz/125 ml) heavy cream
⅔ cup (5 fl oz/150 ml) cane syrup (p. 198)
1 cup (8 fl oz/250 ml) white rhum agricole

Place the bananas and lime juice in a food processor and blend. Add the cream and cane syrup and blend until smooth. Add the rum and place in the refrigerator for 4 hours. Serve well chilled.

PASSION FRUIT PUNCH

This punch is the type of drink you are offered when visiting elderly people. When I used to stay with my grandfather in Marie-Galante or my godmother in the countryside, we often visited older neighbors. Grandmas would open a kitchen cupboard and reveal large bottles of punches like this one. Some of them would have been there for years. My cousins and I would serve it to those sitting around the table playing dominoes or cards. Purists drink it without ice, but when I was old enough to have it, an ice cube mellowed it for me.

Serves 10

6 passion fruits
⅔ cup (5 oz/150 g) raw sugar
1 vanilla pod, cut in half lengthwise
1 bottle (750 ml) white rhum agricole
1 cinnamon stick

Cut the passion fruits in half and scoop out the pulp into a large mixing bowl. Add the sugar, vanilla pod, and rum and stir to mix.

Using a funnel, pour the punch into the empty rum bottle. Insert the cinnamon stick into the bottle. Close the bottle and leave the punch to mature for at least 6 weeks in a cupboard. It will keep for up to 6 months.

Serve in a short glass with two ice cubes.

PEANUT PUNCH

While some settled for coconut punch, my father always took it one step further: peanuts, cocoa – he made punch out of everything! As a child I was allergic to peanuts, so I watched my friends and siblings munch the grilled goodies sold by the roadside with jealousy. I eventually grew out of the allergy, and now I just can't get enough of this punch.

Serves 8

1⅔ cup (9 oz/250 g) peanuts, shelled
1 can (about 14 oz/400 g) condensed milk
1 can (about 14 oz/400 g) evaporated milk
3 pinches grated cinnamon
2 pinches grated nutmeg
½ vanilla pod, split lengthwise
1 bottle (750 ml) white rhum agricole

Put the peanuts, condensed milk, evaporated milk, cinnamon, and nutmeg in a food processor. Using a small knife, scrape the seeds from the vanilla pod into the mixture, then blend to a smooth paste.

Transfer the paste to a large mixing bowl and add the rum. Stir to mix evenly. Using a funnel, pour the punch into the empty rum bottle. Close the bottle and leave the punch in a cupboard away from any light for a week.

Shake well before serving with an ice cube.

PLANTÉ

PLANTEUR

Planteur is as much a tradition as ti' punch (p. 54) in the Caribbean. I was taught from an early age that planteur is the ladylike cocktail to order. It's my mother's favorite. Always on the menu in any local restaurant, it's very mellow and is traditionally based on the principal of balancing various fruit juices with rums of different ages. Angostura bitters is an alcoholic mixer flavored with infused spices and herbs. It's a relatively recent addition, dating back to the 1970s, when the French islands increased their trading links with the rest of the Caribbean. This is my take on planteur.

Serves 6-8

¾ cup (6 fl oz/175 ml) mango juice
scant 1 cup (8 fl oz/225 ml) pineapple
    juice
⅞ cup (7 fl oz/200 ml) guava juice
2 tbsp white rhum agricole
3 tbsp aged rhum agricole
zest of 2 limes, peeled in strips,
    and juice of ½ lime
1½ tsp Angostura bitters
    (approximately 40 drops)
3 tbsp cane syrup (p. 198)
1 cinnamon stick
1 pinch grated nutmeg
3 tbsp grenadine syrup (p. 202)

Put all the fruit juices, rums, lime juice, Angostura bitters, and cane syrup into a large bowl. Stir to mix, then pour into a large jug or two. Add the cinnamon stick, nutmeg, and lime zest. Place in the refrigerator for 2 hours.

To serve, pour a little grenadine syrup into each glass. Pour in the cocktail and add an ice cube.

TIP

You can decorate the cocktail
with finely sliced fresh fruits
such as mango or pineapple.

KOMANSEMAN

STARTERS

◆◆◆◆◆◆◆◆◆◆◆

Creole culture is all about community, and it's perfectly natural for relatives, friends, or neighbors to turn up on your doorstep at any time. Chances are they'll end up in the kitchen, with you whipping up some of these dishes to share. Out comes the *ti' punch*, accompanied by fritters of all sorts (or whatever you have in your refrigerator or cupboard). When you sit down to a big family dinner, you will find not one but four or five of these starters combined in an *assiette créole* (Creole platter). They tend to be light and delicious to pique your appetite for the heavy stuff coming as mains.

If you have a deep-fat fryer for making fritters, awesome. If not, be extremely cautious with the oil. It should be hot, but if it starts to smoke it means it's too hot and the outside of your fritters will burn while the inside won't be cooked. Don't fry with oil that smokes.

FÉROCE D'AVOCAT

AVOCADO FÉROCE (MARTINIQUE)

This was traditionally eaten by workers in the cane and banana fields of Martinique. They would start the day with this filling breakfast, often accompanied by what they called *décollage* or "white coffee" – a small glass of white rum. In recent years this dish has taken a starring role in the *didiko* (Creole brunch).

Serves 4

10 oz (300 g) skinless, boneless
   dried salted cod
1 lime, halved
2 large ripe green avocados
1⅔ cups (7 oz/200 g) coarse
   cassava flour (gari)
¼ onion, very finely chopped
2 garlic cloves, crushed and very
   finely chopped
⅓ Scotch bonnet chile, deseeded and
   very finely chopped
1 sprig parsley, very finely chopped
salt and freshly ground black pepper

Preheat the oven to 475°F (250°C).

Put the saltfish in a saucepan, add cold water to cover, bring to a boil, and boil for 5 minutes. Drain the water.

Put the fish in an ovenproof dish and cook in the oven for 5 minutes. Remove from the oven, cover with cold water, and leave to soak for about 5 minutes.

Drain the water and pat the fish dry with paper towels. Put the fish in the food processor and blend to a fine purée. Squeeze the juice of half a lime over it.

Peel the avocados, chop them into small pieces, and mash them with a fork or potato masher until smooth. Add the cassava flour and mix to a thick paste. Add the fish, onion, garlic, chile, and parsley. Squeeze the other half of the lime over the mixture, then season to taste. Form small balls and serve immediately.

TIP

Gari is a coarse cassava flour
sold in Afro-Caribbean shops.
If you can't find it, replace with
7 oz (200 g) rough oatcakes,
blended in the food processor.

FÉROCE D'AVOCAT

AVOCADO FÉROCE (GUADELOUPE)

Féroce in French (and Creole) means fierce. This Guadeloupe version of the recipe uses a whole hot chile: it is meant to burn and shake you up.

Serves 4

1¼ lb (600 g) skinless, boneless dried salted cod
3 garlic cloves, crushed and very finely chopped
1 onion, very finely chopped
2 green onions, very finely chopped
1 red habanero chile, deseeded and very finely chopped
2 limes
3 tbsp vegetable oil
2 very large ripe green avocados
1⅔ cups (7 oz/200 g) coarse cassava flour (gari), or 7 oz (200 g) rough oatcakes, blended in the food processor

Put the saltfish in a bowl of cold water to soak for 2 hours.

Preheat the oven to 400°F (200°C). Drain the fish, put it in an ovenproof dish, and cook for 10 minutes. Remove from the oven and flake the fish into a bowl. Add the garlic, onion, green onions, and chile and squeeze in the juice of 1 lime. Add the oil and stir.

Wash the avocados, then cut them in half, remove the pits, and scoop out the flesh, ensuring you don't damage the skin. Mash the avocado flesh with a fork and mix in the cassava flour. Add the fish mixture and squeeze in the second lime. Put the mixture back into the avocado shells and serve.

TIP

Chocho salad (p. 98) is ideal
to accompany the féroce.
A simple grated cucumber
also works well.

STARTERS

SALADE DE GOMBOS

CREOLE-STYLE OKRA

Okra, or *gombos* as we call them, were traditionally very common in Creole diets. They now seem to be being consumed less and less. They have a slightly slimy texture but they are very good for you. I loved *gombos* this way. It's so easy to make and works well as a starter or a light dinner for Sunday evening. We consider it a hot salad, but to me it almost feels like a soup; I love slurping the broth.

Serves 4

2 lb (1 kg) fresh okra
1 onion, very finely chopped
4 green onions, very finely chopped
3 sprigs parsley, very finely chopped
2 thyme sprigs
½ Scotch bonnet chile, deseeded
1 pinch baking soda
4 garlic cloves, crushed and very
    finely chopped
juice of 2 limes
salt and freshly ground black pepper

Wash the okra and cut off the tips of the stems. Put them in a saucepan with the onion, green onions, parsley, thyme sprigs, and the half chile. Add water to just cover and add the baking soda. Cover and cook over medium-high heat for 15 minutes.

Using a slotted spoon, lift out the okra into a bowl. Put the saucepan back on the heat and add the garlic, lime juice, and salt and pepper. Reduce over high heat for 2–3 minutes, then pour over the okra. Serve hot.

TIP

Avoid overcooking so the okra isn't too slimy. If you want to make it more like a soup, boil the sauce for only 1 minute after removing the okra.

CRABE FARCI

DRESSED CRAB

This is an essential element in any *assiette créole* (Creole platter). Blue land crab is now a protected species in the French Caribbean, and it is hunted only at specific times of the year. But when the hunting season is open, there are countless ways of cooking it. For this recipe you can boil sea crabs with bay leaves and salt, then pull out the flesh from the claws and legs; you will also need to wash and sterilize the shell before filling it. To save time, I suggest you buy crabmeat from the fishmonger. Serve the crab on its own with salad or as part of a Creole platter with saltfish fritters (p. 76) and fish boudins (p. 80).

Serves 4

¼ baguette (about 2½ oz/70 g), slightly stale is best
3 tbsp low-fat milk
1 onion
2 green onions
3 garlic cloves
2 sprigs parsley
1 sprig thyme, leaves only
½ red habanero (or Scotch bonnet) chile, deseeded
4 tbsp (2 oz/60 g) butter
6 oz (175 g) crabmeat, shredded
juice of 1 lime
salt and freshly ground black pepper
3 tbsp fresh or dried bread crumbs

Preheat the oven to 350°F (180°C). Soak the baguette in the milk for 10 minutes.

Put the onion, green onions, garlic, parsley, thyme, and half chile in a food processor and blend until very finely chopped.

Melt 2 tablespoons of the butter in a frying pan. Add the chopped onion mixture and cook for a minute. Add the crabmeat and lime juice and cook for 2 minutes. Remove from the heat.

Squeeze the milk out of the bread. Put the bread in the food processor and blend to a purée. Add the bread purée to the crab. Put the pan over medium heat and cook for 3–4 minutes, stirring regularly so it doesn't stick to the pan. Season with salt and pepper to taste. Remove from the heat.

Place the stuffing in small ramekins (if you used a whole crab, fill the cleaned shell with the stuffing) and sprinkle the bread crumbs over. Place in the oven for 10 minutes. Serve hot.

CHIKTAY DE MORUE / CHIKTAY LANMORI

SALTFISH CHIQUETAILLE

A classic Creole starter. *Chiquetaille* means "shred." My mother always gets angry with me when she desalts her saltfish and I come into the kitchen to steal large pieces of not-yet-desalted cod and just munch away – I can't resist it. We serve this with cucumber salad and one or two slices of avocado. But sometimes we have it in a baguette for a morning snack or in a *bokit* (p. 100) for dinner.

Serves 4

1¼ lb (600 g) skinless, boneless dried salted cod
2 tbsp sunflower oil
1 onion, very finely chopped
3 green onions, very finely chopped
3 garlic cloves, crushed and very finely chopped
½ red habanero chile, deseeded and very finely chopped
2 sprigs parsley, very finely chopped
1 sprig thyme, leaves only
2 tomatoes, very finely chopped
1 lime

Preheat the oven to 400°F (200°C).

Put the saltfish in a saucepan, add cold water to cover, bring to a boil, and boil for 5 minutes. Drain off the water and repeat the process.

Drain and flake the fish into an ovenproof dish; cook in the oven for 5 minutes. Remove from the oven and flake into a mixing bowl. Add the oil and stir.

Add the onion, green onions, garlic, half chile, parsley, thyme, and tomatoes and mix thoroughly. Add the lime juice, stir, and serve.

TIP

As the saltfish has been thoroughly desalted, you may feel the dish lacks salt; taste and add salt if you wish.

ACCRAS DE MORUE

SALTFISH FRITTERS

My mother is the queen of *accras*. Family and friends can arrive at any time of the day and she whips up some fritters so quickly it's crazy. Her secret is that she always has some desalted saltfish in the freezer in case guests arrive. She doesn't have a deep-fat fryer yet manages to get the oil temperature right every single time.

Makes about 30 fritters

10 oz (300 g) skinless, boneless
    dried salted cod
1 onion, very finely chopped
1 green onion, very
    finely chopped
3 garlic cloves, crushed and
    very finely chopped
2 sprigs parsley, very
    finely chopped
½ Scotch bonnet chile, deseeded
    and very finely chopped
2 eggs, lightly beaten
2¼ cups (9 oz/250 g) self-rising flour
⅔ cup (5 fl oz/150 ml) water
1 quart (32 fl oz/1 liter) sunflower oil

Put the saltfish in a saucepan, add cold water to cover, bring to a boil, and boil for 5 minutes. Drain off the water and repeat the process.

Flake the saltfish really finely into a large bowl. Add the onion, green onion, garlic, parsley, and half chile and mix well. Add the eggs and stir until you have a thick paste. Add the flour and mix well, then add the water to make a rich but lumpy batter.

In a deep pan, heat the oil over medium heat until it reaches 350°F (180°C) or until a cube of bread browns in 3 seconds. Gently drop tablespoonfuls of the batter into the oil and cook for about 30 seconds, turning occasionally, until dark golden brown all over.

Using a slotted spoon, scoop the fritters out of the oil and drain on paper towels. Serve hot with *sauce chien* (p. 190).

ACCRAS DE FRUIT À PAIN

BREADFRUIT FRITTERS

I love breadfruit. This starchy cousin of mulberry is probably my favorite vegetable ever; I can boil it with salt and eat it just like that. These fritters are very delicate, soft and gooey on the inside, a great alternative to traditional fritters.

Makes about 30 fritters

1 breadfruit, about 1¾ lb (800 g)
salt and freshly ground black pepper
2 cups (16 fl oz/500 ml) canned
  coconut milk
1 pinch Colombo powder (p. 41)
2 garlic cloves, crushed and very
  finely chopped
1 sprig thyme, leaves only
3 eggs
juice of 1 lime
4 tbsp (1¾ oz/50 g) all-purpose flour
½ tsp baking powder
1 quart (32 fl oz/1 liter) sunflower oil

Cut the breadfruit in half, remove the core, and peel. Place in a pan of lightly salted boiling water and boil for 45 minutes.

Drain the breadfruit, add the coconut milk, and mash to a purée. Add the Colombo powder, garlic, and thyme. Add the eggs and lime juice and stir to combine. Add the flour and baking powder and stir thoroughly. Season with salt and pepper to taste.

In a deep pan, heat the oil over medium heat until it reaches 350°F (180°C) or until a cube of bread browns in 3 seconds. Gently drop tablespoonfuls of the batter into the oil and cook for about 30 seconds, turning occasionally, until they are deep golden all over.

Using a slotted spoon, scoop the fritters out of the oil and drain on paper towels. Serve hot with a hot spicy sauce, if you like.

TIP

If breadfruit isn't in season, use canned breadfruit and skip the first step.

PRAWN FRITTERS

When one thinks of fritters in the Caribbean, one automatically thinks saltfish. Prawn fritters are probably not quite as popular, but they are super easy to make and finding prawns isn't as difficult as finding saltfish. Just make sure your prawns are very big and juicy.

Makes 20–25 fritters

1 lb (500 g) raw prawns or jumbo
  shrimp
2 garlic cloves: 1 crushed,
  1 very finely chopped
juice of 1 lime
salt and freshly ground black pepper
1¼ cups (7 oz/200 g) all-purpose flour
1 onion, very finely chopped
½ Scotch bonnet chile, deseeded and
  very finely chopped
3 green onions, very finely chopped
1 sprig parsley, very finely chopped
⅔ cup (5 fl oz/150 ml) water
1 egg, lightly beaten
½ tsp baking powder
1 quart (32 fl oz/1 liter) vegetable oil

Peel the prawns and pull off the heads. If they are very big, cut them in half. Put them in a bowl with the crushed garlic clove, lime juice, and salt and pepper and marinate for at least 10 minutes.

Put the flour in a large bowl and make a well in the center. Add the onion, finely chopped garlic, half chile, green onions, and parsley. Add the water and mix to make a batter. Remove the prawns from the marinade, pat them dry, and add them to the batter. Add the egg, mix well, and leave to rest for at least an hour.

Just before frying, add the baking powder and a little more salt and pepper.

In a deep pan, heat the oil over medium heat until it reaches 350°F (180°C) or until a cube of bread browns in 3 seconds. Making sure there is a prawns in every fritter, gently drop teaspoonfuls of the batter into the oil and cook for about 30 seconds, turning occasionally, until they are deep golden all over.

Using a slotted spoon, scoop the fritters out of the oil and drain on paper towels. Serve hot.

RED SNAPPER BOUDINS

Boudins are a Creole institution. The traditional *boudin* is *boudin noir* (black pudding or blood sausage), which is similar to European black puddings but flavored with chiles and herbs. Over time many variations have evolved: crab, saltfish, shrimp ... my favorite style of *boudin* is fish, made with red snapper. For this recipe, it is important that the onions, chile, garlic, and herbs for the sausage filling be chopped extremely finely.

Serves 4-6

1 pack natural sausage casing
  (see Tip, p. 82)
juice of 2 limes
2 lb (1 kg) snapper fillets
2 Scotch bonnet chiles: 1 whole,
  1 deseeded and very finely chopped
4 tbsp vegetable oil
salt and freshly ground black pepper
6 garlic cloves: 1 crushed,
  5 very finely chopped
8 green onions: 2 roughly chopped,
  6 very finely chopped
3 onions: 1 roughly chopped,
  2 very finely chopped
5 sprigs thyme: 2 whole,
  3 very finely chopped
6 sprigs parsley: 2 whole,
  4 very finely chopped
5 bay leaves
1 Caribbean red habanero chile,
  whole (see p. 26)
4 cloves
½ baguette
½ cup (4 fl oz/125 ml) milk
1 tsp ground allspice

Put the sausage casing in a bowl, add cold water to cover and the juice of 1 lime, and leave to soak for at least 30 minutes.

Put the fish in a pan with cold water to just cover, the juice of 1 lime, the whole Scotch bonnet, 2 tablespoons of the oil, and salt and pepper. Bring to a boil, then reduce the heat and simmer gently until the fish is cooked, about 5 minutes. Remove the fish from the poaching broth and set aside to cool.

Next, prepare the broth to cook your boudins: fill a large pot with water and add the crushed garlic clove, the roughly chopped green onions, the roughly chopped onion, whole sprigs of thyme and parsley, the bay leaves, habanero chile, cloves, and salt and pepper. Bring to the simmering point and simmer for at least 30 minutes, taking care that the broth never boils.

Once the fish is cool, flake it as finely as possible with your fingers. Put the baguette in a bowl and soak it with cold water, then squeeze out the water with your hands. Purée the bread using your hands and cover with the milk.

Heat the remaining oil in a large saucepan and cook the finely chopped onions, green onions, chile, and garlic for about 2 minutes. Add the finely chopped thyme, and parsley, the allspice, the fish, and salt and pepper to taste. Cook for 3 minutes. Add the bread and milk and cook for another 3 minutes. The filling should be firm. Leave to cool.

(continued)

Clean the inside of the sausage casing by running water through it using a funnel. Tie one end of the casing. Using a funnel, pour the fish filling into the casing, ensuring you don't pack it in too tightly. Tie the sausages every 4 inches (10 cm) with food-safe string or twist into individual sausages, but do not cut them.

To cook your boudins, hook them over a wooden spoon resting across the top of the pot of broth; they should *never* touch the bottom or sides of the pot, otherwise they will burst. Place your boudins in the broth and cook them over low heat for 15–20 minutes.

Remove the boudins from the pot and leave to cool for about 5 minutes. Cut the individual boudins with scissors and serve with a salad, sliced baguette, or as part of a Creole platter with saltfish fritters (p. 76) and fish boudins (p. 80).

TIP

I use a large sausage casing, the same casing you'd use to make black pudding, which is the ancestor of this recipe. A good butcher will advise you if you say you are making fish sausages that emulate black pudding! Good butchers should sell sausage casing, especially if they make their own sausages. Alternatively, look online. Check the instructions: some need to be soaked for 2 hours before use; some can be kept in the fridge for several months.

GREEN MANGO SOUSKAÏ

I love green mangoes; the sour taste works fabulously with chile and lime. This is a classic from Martinique. *Souskaï* is the name of both the dish and the technique of macerating fruits in a savory vinaigrette of lime, garlic, salt, and chile. If you like, you can add some diced fresh pineapple.

Serves 4

2 large green mangoes
1 garlic clove, crushed and very
   finely chopped
2 red bird's-eye chiles,
   very finely chopped
juice of 3 limes
1 tbsp sunflower oil
2 sprigs parsley, finely chopped
salt

Peel the mangoes with a potato peeler (this will ensure you don't waste any of the flesh). Coarsely grate the flesh into a mixing bowl. Add the garlic, chiles, lime juice, oil, and parsley. Add salt to taste and stir. Cover with plastic wrap and leave in the refrigerator for at least 1 hour before serving.

TIP

You can buy green mangoes
from Asian markets and grocery
shops. If you can't find them, use
an unripe mango from your local
supermarket: the flesh will be harder,
even if there's sweetness to it.

TARTE À LA MORUE

SALTFISH TART

In every Caribbean household you will find a piece of saltfish hidden somewhere in a cupboard or, in my mum's case, in the freezer. It's just one of the ingredients that, across the region, people invariably use. Although fritters are the most well-known usage, saltfish tart is a common feature of the Creole table, especially at a *didiko* (Creole brunch) or for dinner on Sunday when not having soup.

Serves 4–6

4 tbsp sunflower oil, plus extra
 for greasing
14 oz (400 g) skinless, boneless
 dried salted cod
4 onions, very finely chopped
5 garlic cloves, crushed and
 very finely chopped
½ Scotch bonnet chile, very finely
 chopped
2 sprigs parsley, very finely chopped
2 sprigs thyme, leaves only
juice of 1 lime
1¼ cups (10 fl oz/300 ml)
 crème fraîche
2 eggs
flour, for dusting
7 oz (200 g) prepared pie dough
5 oz (150 g) Gruyère cheese, grated

Preheat the oven to 350°F (180°C). Line a 10½-inch (26-cm) fluted tart pan with parchment paper and brush lightly with oil.

Put the saltfish in a saucepan, add cold water to cover, bring to a boil, and boil for 5 minutes. Drain and leave to cool. Flake the fish.

Heat 2 tablespoons of the oil in a frying pan and cook the onions, garlic, half chile, parsley, and thyme until softened. Add the flaked fish, lime juice, and the remaining oil and cook for 2 minutes.

In a mixing bowl, beat the crème fraîche with the eggs. Add the fish mixture and mix to combine.

On a lightly floured surface, roll out the dough and line the prepared tart pan. Prick the pastry all over with a fork. Place it in the oven for 2–3 minutes.

Remove the pastry shell from the oven and pour in the fish mixture. Sprinkle the cheese on top and return to the oven until golden and cooked, 25 minutes. Serve hot.

TIP

If you have small tartlet pans, make individual tartlets instead and serve with salad for a light dinner.

CREOLE MEAT PIES

These little meat pies are seen at *every* party throughout the Christmas season. Traditionally they are made with pork, as are most of the savory foods eaten during that time. However, nowadays these little pies are something we enjoy all year round, filled with saltfish, beef, or even conch, and you'll see them in bakeries and at markets.

Makes 20 small pies

2 tbsp sunflower oil
7 oz (200 g) ground pork or beef
2 garlic cloves, very finely chopped
½ red habanero chile,
    very finely chopped
3 green onions, very finely chopped
3 sprigs thyme, leaves only,
    very finely chopped
2 sprigs parsley, very finely chopped
½ tsp ground allspice
½ tsp pumpkin pie spice
salt and freshly ground black pepper
flour, for dusting
10 oz (300 g) chilled puff pastry dough
1 egg yolk, beaten with 1 tsp low-fat
    milk

Preheat the oven to 350°F (180°C). Line a large baking sheet (or two smaller ones) with parchment paper.

Heat the oil in a frying pan over medium-high heat and brown the meat. Add the garlic, half chile, green onions, thyme, parsley, allspice, pumpkin pie spice, and salt and pepper and cook for 2–3 minutes. Leave to cool slightly.

Divide the pastry into 4 pieces. On a lightly floured work surface, roll out the first piece of pastry until it is 1/16 inch (2 mm) thick. Using a 4-inch (10-cm) round cutter (or a small glass), cut out 10 circles. Place the pastry circles on the lined baking sheet. Put 1 tablespoon of the filling in the middle of each circle; don't overfill. Cover it with another pastry circle. Using the tines of a fork, crimp the edges of the pastry. Repeat until you've used all the pastry and filling.

Using a pastry brush, generously brush egg yolk all over the top of the pies. Bake in the oven until golden brown, 20 minutes. Serve hot or cold.

QUEUE DE LANGOUSTE FRIT

FRIED LOBSTER

Lobster never used to be posh food in the Caribbean. My grandfather owned a number of boats, so my mother knew everything about the sea and its food. She tells me that lobsters used to be given away for free by fishermen, since they got caught in their nets and weren't seen as being of value. Today lobster is very sought after and catching it is highly regulated as it is becoming increasingly rare. When it's in season you'll find simple charcoal-grilled lobster in the islands' restaurants; this recipe is a quick and easy alternative to try at home.

Serves 4

4 raw lobster tails, peeled
3 limes: 1 squeezed, 2 cut into wedges
3 garlic cloves, crushed and
  very finely chopped
1 Scotch bonnet chile,
  very finely chopped
2 sprigs thyme, leaves only
salt and freshly ground black pepper
1 egg
1 tbsp coconut milk
4 tbsp cayenne pepper
1 tbsp allspice
1 cup (5 oz/150 g) fine cornmeal
2 cups (16 fl oz/500 ml) sunflower oil
hot Creole sauce (p. 190; optional)

Marinate the lobster tails with the juice of 1 lime, the garlic, chile, thyme, and salt and pepper for at least an hour.

Cut the lobster tails into ¾-inch (2-cm) pieces and pat dry with paper towels. In a bowl, beat the egg with the coconut milk. In another bowl, mix the cayenne pepper with the allspice. Place the cornmeal in another bowl.

Heat the oil in a frying pan over medium heat.

Coat the lobster pieces in the beaten egg, then the cayenne, then in cornmeal. Place them gently into the hot oil and fry, turning with tongs or a slotted spoon, until golden, 2 minutes. Drain on paper towels. Serve immediately, with lime wedges or hot Creole sauce, if you like.

TIP

If lobster is not availble,
you can make this recipe
with peeled jumbo shrimp.

COCONUT SLAW

Coconut is my favorite fruit in the world. I love it because it's so versatile: from starter to dessert, the possibilities are endless. I created this recipe because I love coconut *souskay* – a traditional Martinique recipe – but always felt it lacked something, a bit of a kick, creaminess, texture... this recipe is one of my guests' favorites, always on the request list for menus at my supper clubs. Serve with smoked herring *chiquetaille* (p. 92).

Serves 4

1 coconut
¼ carrot, coarsely grated
1-inch (2.5-cm) piece fresh ginger, finely grated
¼ Scotch bonnet chile, very finely chopped (optional)
salt
1 lime
4 tbsp coconut milk

Break the husk of the coconut and scoop out the meat. Wash the meat and pat dry with paper towels. Coarsely grate the coconut meat into a mixing bowl.

Add the carrot, ginger, and chile (if using) and season with salt to taste. Squeeze in the lime juice, add the coconut milk, and stir to mix evenly. Cover with plastic wrap and place in the refrigerator for 1 hour before serving.

CHIKTAY D'HARENG SAUR

SMOKED HERRING CHIQUETAILLE

Whenever I go home and my mum asks me what I want her to make, I request smoked herring. She doesn't understand why. I like the saltiness, the smoky taste, the dryness of the flesh. This is very easy to make, and I love it on a slice of baguette griddled with olive oil, with finely chopped tomatoes and fresh arugula, bruschetta style (pictured, p. 91).

Serves 4

2 smoked herring
1 lime, halved
1 sprig thyme
1 or 2 Caribbean red habanero
  chiles (optional)
1 onion, chopped
3 garlic cloves, crushed
2 sprigs parsley
2 tbsp sunflower oil

First prepare your herring: slice the belly of the fish open and check if there is an egg pocket; if so, discard it. Clean the fish in cold water, then put them in a saucepan, add cold water to cover, bring to a boil, and boil for 5 minutes.

Drain off the water and cover with fresh cold water, add the juice of half a lime and the thyme, and a whole chile, if you like. Boil for another 5 minutes.

Drain the herring and remove the flesh from the bones, taking care to pick out every single bone. Flake the fish with your fingertips until it is completely shredded.

Blitz the onion, garlic, parsley, and a chile (if using) in a food processor and add to the herring.

Squeeze in the rest of the lime, stir, add the oil, and stir again, then serve.

TIP

For a party, you could serve this stuffed in tomatoes, having scooped out their flesh. Cherry tomatoes look and taste great.

CROQUETTES D'IGNAME

YAM CROQUETTES

Yams are one of those things that were part of my diet growing up in the Caribbean but aren't always the most exciting to cook with. Yam gratin and boiled yam were the two ways we had them regularly. These croquettes are my way of making yam a tad more exciting, with an interesting flavor combination that includes coconut.

Serves 4

1 lb (500 g) yellow yam (true yam)
3 tbsp coconut milk
1 egg, lightly beaten
1 sprig parsley, very finely chopped
1 sprig thyme, leaves only
1 green onion, very finely chopped
¼ Scotch bonnet chile,
   very finely chopped
1 garlic clove, very finely chopped
1½ tbsp (¾ oz/20 g) butter, at room
   temperature
salt and freshly ground black pepper
4 tbsp (1½ oz/45 g) all-purpose flour
2 cups (16 fl oz/500 ml) vegetable oil

Peel the yam, then cut it into 1-inch (2.5-cm) pieces and boil until soft when pierced with a knife. Drain and mash the yam with a fork, adding the coconut milk to make a coarse purée. Stir in the egg, herbs, green onion, chile, and garlic. Add the butter and season with salt and pepper to taste.

Shape the mixture into balls the size of an egg, roll them in flour, and flatten them between the palms of your hands.

Heat the oil in a frying pan over medium heat. Place the fritters gently into the hot oil and panfry, turning once, until browned on both sides. Drain on paper towels. Serve hot, with a salad.

TIP

Yellow and white yams look similar on the outside, although yellow yam tends to be more hairy, so the best thing to do is ask the shopkeeper for yellow yam. If yellow yams are not available, you can substitute white yams or sweet potatoes.

CHOCHO GRATIN

This classic of Creole cuisine makes a rather bland squash taste delicious: the watery flesh takes on new life when mixed with bacon. Be very gentle with the chocho skin, as it breaks quite easily.

Serves 4

2 large chochos (chayotes/
  christophines)
salt and freshly ground black pepper
1 tbsp sunflower oil
1 tbsp butter
6 oz (175 g) smoked bacon,
  cut into lardons
1 onion, very finely chopped
3 green onions, very finely chopped
1 garlic clove, crushed and very
  finely chopped
1 sprig parsley, chopped
3 tbsp crème fraîche
1 pinch pumpkin pie spice
1 oz (30 g) Emmentaler cheese, grated

Cut the chochos in half and remove the cores. Place the squash in a pan of lightly salted boiling water and boil until the flesh is very soft, 45 minutes. Drain and leave to cool.

Preheat the oven to 350°F (180°C).

Using a knife, gently remove the fibrous part around the center of the chochos. Using a spoon, gently scoop out the flesh, leaving the skin intact. Mash the flesh with a potato masher or a fork and set aside.

Heat the oil and butter in a frying pan over medium-high heat and cook the bacon, onion, green onions, garlic, and parsley until the onion has softened.

Add the chocho flesh, crème fraîche, pumpkin pie spice, and most of the cheese, and season with salt and pepper to taste.

Place the chocho skins in a baking dish and fill them with the stuffing. Sprinkle the remaining cheese on top. Place in the oven for about 15 minutes, until golden. Serve hot.

TIP

These squash are slightly large,
but can be served as part
of a Creole platter.

CREOLE COCKTAIL SAUSAGES

Who doesn't have frankfurters in their cupboard in Guadeloupe and Martinique? It's not gourmet food and it comes from a can, but in the Caribbean, people just turn up on your doorstep unannounced. That's part of the culture. This recipe could save your (social) life. You'll often find this on the table when friends and family have come round to say hi and ended up spending hours chatting on the terrace with the fan on and some lemongrass candles to send the mosquitoes away.

Serves 4

1 can or vacuum pack (about 12 oz/
    350 g) cocktail frankfurters
4 tbsp sunflower oil
1 onion, very finely chopped
2 green onions, chopped
3 garlic cloves, crushed
1 cup (8 fl oz/250 ml) water
2 sprigs thyme
1 Scotch bonnet chile, sliced in rings
1 bay leaf
salt and freshly ground black pepper

Cut the frankfurters into slices ½ inch (12 mm) thick. Cook the frankfurters in a frying pan with 2 tablespoons of the oil over medium heat for 2 minutes. Add the onion, green onions, garlic, and the remaining oil and cook for about 3 minutes more.

Add the water, the thyme, chile, bay leaf, and salt and pepper and cook over low heat for 5 minutes.

Serve in a bowl with cocktail picks.

CUCUMBER AND SARDINE SALAD

This is the ultimate beach food. When you decide to head to the beach for the day with friends, you need simple delicious food you can whip up right there on the beach. In the Caribbean, canned food can be a lifesaver in the hurricane season, when there are power cuts and we can't get to the shops. Some canned foods, such as sardines, have become part of our traditions. Serve with slices of warm baguette.

Serves 4

1 cucumber
two 1¾-oz (50-g) cans sardines in
   sunflower oil, drained
½ lime
2 garlic cloves, crushed
2 sprigs parsley, very finely chopped
1 red habanero chile, very finely
   chopped
salt and freshly ground black pepper
1 tbsp coconut oil (optional)

Peel the cucumber and coarsely grate it into a serving bowl. Drain off as much liquid as possible.

Put the sardines in a bowl and shred, using a fork. Squeeze the lime over the sardines. Add the garlic, parsley, chile, and salt and pepper to taste.

Put the sardine mixture in a layer on top of the cucumber and pour the coconut oil, if using, over the top.

CHOCHO SALAD

Many of my students arrive at my classes saying they hate chocho (if they have had it before). They have childhood memories of chocho in a slimy soup or boiled with no seasoning. This recipe never fails to reconcile them with chocho. It's just a simple salad, but most people don't even know you can eat it raw. Once they've tried this, it becomes a go-to recipe when they want an alternative to their usual salads.

Serves 4

2 chochos (chayotes/christophines)
juice of 1 lime
salt and freshly ground black
  pepper
2 tbsp sunflower oil
1 garlic clove, very finely chopped
¼ Scotch bonnet chile, deseeded
  and very finely chopped

Peel the chochos with a potato peeler and cut them in half. Grate the flesh and stop grating once you reach the core. Throw away the core.

In a bowl, make a vinaigrette with the lime juice, salt, pepper, oil, garlic, and chile.

Cover the chochos with the vinaigrette and toss gently. Place in the refrigerator for at least 15 minutes before serving.

BOKIT AU CORNED BEEF

CORNED BEEF MINI BOKITS

This is what I call a "hard times recipe." Processed meat and fried dough wouldn't strike anyone as gourmet food, but they are delicious. This is the type of food you'd cook if you were trapped in your house during a hurricane or in the aftermath of a flood from a tropical downpour.

Makes 15–20 mini bokits

Bokits
½ tbsp instant yeast
1 tsp salt
3 tbsp milk
⅞ cup (7 fl oz/200 ml) water
3 cups plus 2 tbsp (12 oz/375 g)
 all-purpose flour, plus extra
 for dusting
vegetable oil for greasing

Filling
3 tbsp vegetable oil
1 can (about 12 oz/350 g) corned beef
 (canned pressed beef), chopped
1 onion, very finely chopped
1 green onion, very finely chopped
3 garlic cloves, crushed and
 very finely chopped
1 Scotch bonnet chile, deseeded and
 very finely chopped
2 sprigs thyme, leaves only
2 sprigs parsley, very finely chopped
1 tbsp white vinegar
salt and freshly ground black pepper

1 quart (32 fl oz/1 liter) vegetable oil

To make the bokits, in a small bowl, dissolve the yeast and the salt in the milk. Pour the yeasty milk into a large mixing bowl and add the water and flour. Knead for at least 10 minutes, until the dough is smooth and elastic. Shape into a ball, place in an oiled bowl, cover, and leave in a warm place to rise for at least 5 hours.

To make the filling, heat the oil in a frying pan over medium-high heat. Add the corned beef and cook for about 2 minutes. Add the onion, green onion, garlic, chile, thyme, and parsley and cook, stirring frequently, until thoroughly cooked and slightly crisp, 3–4 minutes.

Add the vinegar and stir to deglaze the pan. Add salt and pepper to taste, cook for another minute, and then remove from the heat.

To shape the bokits, pinch off a small ball of dough about 2 inches (5 cm) wide and ¹⁄₁₆ inch (2 mm) thick. On a lightly floured work surface, roll out the dough to a thin circle about 6 inches (15 cm) in diameter. Place 2 tablespoons of the corned beef mixture on one side of the circle and fold the other half over the corned beef. Press down the edges. Repeat until you have used all the filling.

In a deep pan, heat the oil over medium heat until it reaches 350°F (180°C) or until a cube of bread browns in 3 seconds. Gently lower a bokit into the oil and cook until golden and crisp, about 1 minute on each side. Scoop out of the oil and drain on paper towels. Eat while still hot.

PWASSON É FWIDMÈ
FISH AND SEAFOOD

◆◆◆◆◆◆◆◆◆◆

Caribbean Creole cuisine showcases its diverse influences in the arena of main dishes, which we call *pla'*. Some of the recipes are seasonal because of the availability of the ingredients, some because they are so closely linked to specific holidays. Others are invariably consumed at least once a week in Creole households.

Fish and seafood tend to dominate, in many forms: stewed, grilled, fried, poached, and cooked in rice – you're spoiled for choice. The Amerindian heritage is seen in the grilled fish and seafood, the influence of the French in the fragrant broths used for poaching. Saltfish was introduced by the Portuguese – and there are rice dishes that will remind you of Spanish paella. *Dombrés* (see p. 118), or dumplings, are a truly Creole creation, evolving at a time when slaves and field workers needed energy-rich foods to add to whatever fish or meat they could get their hands on.

BLAFF D'OUASSOUS

PRAWN BLAFF

Some say blaff gets its name from the sound fish and seafood make when thrown into the fragrant broth: "blaff!" Others think it derives from the French word *blafard*, which means pale, because of how colorless the sauce is. This simple dish has its roots in French cuisine, with a very aromatic broth that tastes wonderful served with simply boiled roots such as sweet potatoes, yam, or plantains.

Serves 4

2 lb (1 kg) raw prawns or jumbo shrimp
2 limes
3 garlic cloves, crushed
salt and freshly ground black pepper
2 tbsp sunflower oil
2 onions, chopped
1 clove
3 green onions, chopped
1 bay leaf
2 sprigs thyme, leaves only
2 cups (16 fl oz/500 ml) water
1 habanero chile
2 sprigs parsley, chopped

Marinate the prawns in their shells with the juice of 1 lime, 1 crushed garlic clove, salt, and pepper for at least 2 hours.

Heat the oil in a pot over medium heat, add the onions, clove, green onions, bay leaf, and thyme and cook for 3 minutes. Add the water, the whole chile, and juice of ½ lime and cook for 5 minutes, stirring occasionally, taking care not to burst the chile.

Add the prawns with their marinade along with the remaining garlic, juice of ½ lime, parsley, and salt and pepper to taste. Cover and cook for another 5 minutes. Remove the chile and serve hot in bowls.

FLAMBÉ PRAWNS

I've always loved the wow factor of flambé. It mesmerized me the first day I was allowed to flambé food, which happened to be prawns, so this is a milestone recipe for me.

Serves 4–6

2 lb (1 kg) raw prawns or jumbo
    shrimp
juice of 1 lime
5 tbsp (2½ fl oz/75 ml) white rum
4 tbsp vegetable oil
1 onion, sliced
2 garlic cloves, crushed
2 sprigs parsley, finely chopped
1 sprig thyme, leaves only
1 bay leaf
salt and freshly ground black pepper
2 tbsp brown sugar
4 tbsp aged rum

Marinate the prawns with the lime juice, half the white rum, 2 tablespoons of the oil, the onion, garlic, parsley, thyme, bay leaf, salt, and pepper for at least 2 hours.

Thread the prawns onto small skewers.

Heat the remaining 2 tablespoons oil in a large frying pan over medium heat and cook the prawns for 2–3 minutes on each side.

Sprinkle the sugar over the prawns and – standing well back as the flames leap up – immediately pour in the remaining white rum and the aged rum and flambé, either by tilting the pan (if you have a gas range) or by holding a match near to the pan (on an electric range). As soon as the flames die down, slide the prawns off the skewers onto a serving platter and pour the rum sauce over. Serve immediately.

OCTOPUS FRICASSÉE

The local variety of octopus in the seas of Guadeloupe and Martinique is called *chatrou*. If you ask for anything else, they won't know what you're talking about. When I was growing up, my father cooked this dish just for me, since none of my siblings nor my mother like it. I love it with plain boiled white rice and a large piece of chile on the side. I'll never get enough!

Serves 4

2 lb (1 kg) octopus, gutted, cleaned, and beak removed
3 limes
salt and freshly ground black pepper
3 garlic cloves, crushed and very finely chopped
2 sprigs thyme
1 large bay leaf
4 tbsp sunflower oil
1 onion, very finely chopped
4 green onions, very finely chopped
2 cloves
1 habanero chile
3 large ripe tomatoes, chopped
⅞ cup (7 fl oz/200 ml) water
2 sprigs parsley, chopped
stewed red kidney beans (p. 168), for serving
boiled basmati rice, for serving

Rinse the octopus thoroughly in water. Use some newspaper to clean it and remove all the slime. Ensure you get rid of all the ink. Squeeze a lime over the octopus. Wrap the octopus in plastic wrap and pound it with a mallet or a rolling pin (or the bottom of a heavy saucepan) for about 5 minutes.

Cut the octopus into chunky 1½-inch (4-cm) pieces and marinate with salt, pepper, the juice of half a lime, 1 garlic clove, 1 sprig of thyme, and 1 bay leaf. Place in the refrigerator for at least 2 hours, or preferably overnight.

Heat 3 tablespoons of the oil in a pot over medium heat, add the octopus and its marinade, and cook it for a few minutes until it releases a pinkish liquid. Add the remaining 2 garlic cloves, the onion, green onions, cloves, and 1 sprig of thyme and cook, covered, over low heat for 10 minutes.

Add the juice of 1 lime and the whole chile, tomatoes, and water. Cover and cook over medium heat for 25 minutes.

Once the liquid has reduced slightly, add 1 tablespoon oil and the parsley. Taste and adjust the seasoning. Add the juice of half a lime, cover the pot, and cook over high heat for 5 minutes. Stir occasionally, taking care not to burst the chile.

Remove the chile. Serve ho, with stewed beans and rice.

LOBSTER FRICASSÉE

I love lobster. It's hard to believe that back when tourism wasn't so developed in Guadeloupe and Martinique, fishermen would offer lobsters free or give them to customers instead of charge. Nowadays, lobster is synonymous with a fancy meal when you have something to celebrate.

Serves 4

2 lb (1 kg) raw lobster tails with
  shell on
2 limes
salt and freshly ground black pepper
3 tbsp sunflower oil
1 onion, very finely chopped
2 green onions, very finely chopped
2 sprigs thyme
2 sprigs parsley, chopped
2 pinches ground allspice
1 bay leaf
2 garlic cloves, crushed
3 ripe tomatoes, chopped
1 tbsp tomato paste
½ cup (4 fl oz/125 ml) water
1 Scotch bonnet chile
boiled rice, for serving

Marinate the lobster tails with the juice of 1 lime, salt, and pepper for at least an hour.

Lift the lobster out of its marinade and pat dry. Heat the oil in a pot over medium heat, add the lobster, and cook for 3–4 minutes. Add the onion, green onions, thyme sprigs, parsley, allspice, bay leaf, and garlic and cook for an additional 3–4 minutes.

Add the tomatoes and tomato paste and stir. Season with salt and pepper to taste and add the water, the whole chile, and the juice of 1 lime. Cover and cook over low heat for 30 minutes, stirring occasionally, taking care not to burst the chile.

Remove the chile and thyme. Serve hot with rice.

FISH COURT BOUILLON

Creole fish court bouillon is the recipe every cook in the Caribbean has to master. It's a tomato-based, very spicy broth in which parrotfish, snapper, and other colorful Caribbean fish are poached until tender. It can be made with just one type of fish or a mix of different fish.

Most cooks in the French Caribbean keep some achiote seeds in a bottle of vegetable oil to use for fish court bouillon. The seeds give the oil a subtle peppery, nutty flavor and a warm red color. Unrefined palm oil can be used instead; it has a reddish color but a slightly different taste. Serve hot with root vegetables or ground provisions (p. 40), which could include boiled plantains, yams, breadfruit, or sweet potatoes.

Serves 4

2 lb (1 kg) red snapper, whole parrotfish, red butterfish, or pink sea bream steaks, scaled and cleaned
3 garlic cloves, crushed
1 bay leaf
3 limes
salt and freshly ground black pepper
1 tbsp sunflower oil
1 cup (8 fl oz/250 ml) water
3 tbsp achiote-infused oil or unrefined palm oil
1 onion, very finely chopped
3 sprigs thyme
3 sprigs parsley, chopped
3 green onions, very finely chopped
3 large ripe tomatoes, chopped
2 tbsp tomato paste
1 Scotch bonnet chile

If using parrotfish or any other small fish, leave them whole. If using red snapper, cut them in half. In a large mixing bowl, combine 1 garlic clove, the bay leaf, the juice of 2 limes, salt and pepper, the sunflower oil, and half of the water. Add all the fish and marinate for at least 2 hours.

Heat the achiote oil in a large pot over medium heat and cook the onion, thyme sprigs, parsley, green onions, and the remaining garlic for about a minute. Add the tomatoes and cook for 2 minutes. Add the remaining water and stir in the tomato paste. Cook for another 2 minutes.

Add the fish and marinade to the pot. They will cook at different times, so add firmer and larger fish first, smaller fish last. Ensure the sauce covers them; if not, add more water. Add the whole chile. Cover the pot and cook over low heat for 10 minutes for most small fish, 15 minutes for snapper, and 20 minutes if using sea bream steak.

Season with salt and pepper to taste. Remove the chile and bay leaf.

GREEN BANANA AND SALTFISH

I love the simplicity of this dish. In Guadeloupe the people you'll see ordering this for their lunch are often the big guys: truck drivers, builders, people with tough jobs working under the very hot Caribbean sun. Ti' punch (p. 54) is de rigueur with this dish. It's a rustic everyday meal, served in large portions – one of my favorites.

Serves 4

4 thick salted cod cutlets
8 green bananas
6 tablespoons sunflower oil
2–3 garlic cloves, crushed
1 bay leaf
4 sprigs thyme
2 sprigs parsley, chopped
juice of 1½ limes
1 habanero chile, deseeded
    and finely chopped
¼ cup (2 fl oz/60 ml) water
2 onions, sliced
salt and freshly ground black pepper
1 large cucumber, peeled and grated
1 large avocado

Put the salted cod in a saucepan, add cold water to cover, bring to a boil, and boil for 5 minutes. Drain off the water and repeat the process. Drain.

Wash the green bananas thoroughly. Cut off both ends and make a lengthwise slit ⅜ inch (1 cm) deep; once boiled, the skin will drop off easily. Boil the green bananas for 30 minutes.

Meanwhile, heat 2 tablespoons oil in a wide, shallow pot over medium heat. Add the cod and cook for about 2 minutes on each side. Add the garlic, bay leaf, thyme sprigs, parsley, juice of 1 lime, and half of the chile and cook for 5 minutes. Reduce the heat to low and add the water. Cook for 5 minutes, then set aside.

In a frying pan, heat 4 tablespoons oil over medium heat, add the onions, and cook for about 10 minutes, until they become translucent. Add a little salt to taste, a pinch of pepper, and the remaining chile. Tip the onions over the cod.

Squeeze the juice of half a lime over the cucumbers. Peel the avocado and cut into small cubes.

Drain the green bananas and serve on a plate with the cod, cucumber, and avocado.

TIP

Traditionally, we like to have a habanero chile and a lime wedge on the side to adjust the flavors to individual taste and some sunflower oil to pour over the green bananas. We crush everything together, from the fish to the avocado, and although it's a messy plate, the flavors combine perfectly.

HACHIS D'IGNAME ET DE MORUE

CREOLE PARMENTIER: YAM AND SALTFISH

My father was anti-potatoes. It was almost like a vendetta. Potatoes were not likely to have grown on our ground, so he felt we should use local roots instead. We did have potatoes from time to time, but yams would have been his first choice. He planted them in our garden, and they were massive. This is one way we'd have them.

Serves 4–6

2 lb (1 kg) true yam
salt and freshly ground black pepper
3 tbsp butter, at room temperature,
  plus extra for greasing
4 tbsp sunflower oil
1 onion, very finely chopped
3 green onions, very finely chopped
4 garlic cloves, crushed
6 tbsp (3 fl oz/100 ml) canned
  coconut milk
10 oz (300 g) saltfish chiquetaille
  (p. 75)
5 tbsp fresh or dried bread crumbs
4 oz (125 g) Emmentaler cheese,
  grated

Peel the yam and cut into chunks. Place in a pan of lightly salted boiling water and boil for 30 minutes. Drain and mash.

Preheat the oven to 350°F (180°C). Butter a large gratin dish.

Heat the oil in a saucepan over medium heat, add the onion, green onions, and garlic and cook until softened. Add the yam purée and stir to mix, then add the coconut milk, butter, and salt and pepper to taste.

Spread half of the yam purée over the bottom of the gratin dish, cover with the saltfish chiquetaille, and then with the rest of the yam purée. Sprinkle the bread crumbs and cheese evenly over the surface. Bake for about 15 minutes, until the top is golden. Serve hot.

BLAFF DE POISSON

FISH BLAFF

"Blaff." That's the sound fish makes when you drop it into the broth. This is so simple. It is one of the first recipes I ever learned to make, when I was around eight years old. Water, herbs, spices, and fish. Anyone can do this.

Serves 4

2 lb (1 kg) fish, such as pink sea bream
   or red mullet, scaled and cleaned
4 garlic cloves, crushed
5 bay leaves
juice of 6 limes
salt and freshly ground black pepper
2 tbsp sunflower oil
1 onion, sliced
3 green onions, chopped
3 sprigs thyme
3 sprigs parsley, chopped
1 Scotch bonnet chile
2 cups (16 fl oz/500 ml) water

Marinate the fish with 2 of the garlic cloves, 2 bay leaves, the juice of 4 limes, and salt and pepper for at least 2 hours.

Heat the oil in a pot over medium heat, add the onion, the remaining garlic, green onions, thyme sprigs, parsley, the remaining 3 bay leaves, the whole chile, and salt and pepper and cook for 2 minutes. Add the water and bring to the simmering point. Add the fish and the juice of 2 limes and simmer for 15 minutes.

Taste and adjust the seasoning, remove the chile, and serve hot, in bowls, ideally with boiled plantains.

COCONUT MILK RED SNAPPER

I love fish. Growing up on an island that is known for its beautiful seas and outstanding coral life, I have many memories of going to the market with my father very early in the morning and buying fish that was still alive in the fishermen's boat. Although they were happy to scale and clean the fish, my father insisted that my brother and I do this so we would learn how to prepare it. It was an exciting learning curve for me to understand the anatomy of the different fish – and it really made me appreciate how wonderful fish can be.

Serves 4

4 small red snapper, scaled, cleaned,
   and filleted
salt and freshly ground black pepper
5 green onions, very finely chopped
1 onion, very finely chopped
½ Scotch bonnet chile,
   very finely chopped
3 garlic cloves, crushed and very
   finely chopped
2 limes
2 tbsp sunflower oil
⅞ cup (7 fl oz/200 ml) canned
   coconut milk
2 tbsp finely chopped parsley

Cut the snapper fillets into thin strips and place them in a bowl. Season with salt and pepper. Add the green onions, onion, chile, and garlic. Squeeze 2 limes over the fish. Using your hands, mix the fish gently with the marinade. Cover and leave in the refrigerator for at least 3 hours.

Take the bowl out of the refrigerator 10 minutes before you are ready to serve.

Heat the oil in a frying pan over medium-high heat. Remove the fish from the marinade and pat dry with paper towels. Put the snapper into the oil and cook for 2 minutes on each side.

Add the coconut milk to the pan and cook for 2 minutes.

Divide the fish among four plates, pour some of the coconut milk over, and sprinkle with chopped parsley.

DOMBRÉS AND PRAWNS

This is my go-to recipe. It's quick, it's delicious, and the ingredients are easy to find. Even when I was a student in a studio flat with the most basic kitchenette, I managed to make this in a small saucepan. It instantly takes me home. It's my ultimate comfort dish.

Serves 4

2 tbsp vegetable oil
14 oz (400 g) raw prawns or jumbo
   shrimp in their shells
3 green onions, chopped
1 large onion, very finely chopped
1 tomato, diced
1 can (14 oz/400 g) chopped tomatoes
2 garlic cloves, crushed
3 cups (24 fl oz/700 ml) water
3 pinches salt
Dombré dough, rolled into small balls
   (p. 41)
juice of 1 lime
1 Scotch bonnet chile
3 sprigs parsley, chopped

Heat the oil in a large pot over medium heat. Throw in the prawns and cook until pink.

Add the green onions and onion and cook for about 5 minutes, until softened.

Add the fresh tomato, canned tomatoes, and garlic and cook for 5 minutes.

Add the water and salt and bring to the simmering point. Add the dombrés to the sauce. Squeeze in the lime juice, add the whole chile, cover the pan, and cook over low heat until the sauce thickens, 30 minutes.

Remove the chile, add the chopped parsley, and serve.

CRAB MATÉTÉ

Easter is one of the biggest celebrations in the French Caribbean. My father used to start preparing for the Easter feast from the first week of Lent. We would go to Morne à l'Eau – a small town in Guadeloupe renowned as the place where you can get the best crabs – and would buy about 15 of them. We farmed the crabs for a month, feeding them chiles, green onions, garlic, and parsley. This flavored them from within, ensuring the flesh was as tasty as could be.

From crabmeat rum punch to crab matété, crab callaloo, and dombrés and crab, crabs are at the center of the celebrations. There's even a traditional Creole song about the benefits of crab matété, claiming it is where Creole men get their "strength." In Guadeloupe you say *matété* and in Martinique *matoutou*—different names, same delicious rice dish.

The indigenous people of the islands are known to have eaten land crabs in various ways. One of their recipes used a sauce of boiled cassava juice, hot peppers, tomatoes, and the fat from the crab's head. The ancestor of today's matété?

Serves 4

4 fresh whole crabs, or 12 crab claws
3 limes
4 large garlic cloves, crushed and very finely chopped
2 Scotch bonnet chiles, deseeded and very finely chopped
salt and freshly ground black pepper
4 tbsp vegetable oil
3 slices smoked bacon, cut into small cubes, or 10 oz (300 g) smoked bacon, cut into lardons
1 large onion, very finely chopped
2 green onions, very finely chopped
2 sprigs parsley, chopped
2 sprigs thyme
4 large ripe tomatoes, diced
3 cloves
2 bay leaves
1 tsp Colombo powder (p. 41)
1⅓ cups (8 oz/250 g) long-grain rice, washed twice

Clean your crabs with a small scrubbing brush. If using whole crabs, pull the shells away from the bodies. Discard the shells, the small stomach sac just behind the crab's mouth, and the soft gray gills. Cut one of the limes into quarters. Clean the bodies with cold water and use the juice of ¼ lime to clean each crab, rubbing the squeezed lime wedge over the body. Using a heavy knife, chop the crab bodies into quarters, keeping two or three legs attached to each quarter. Marinate the crab pieces or claws with the juice of 1 lime, 1 garlic clove, 1 chile, and salt and pepper. Place in the refrigerator for at least 4 hours.

Heat 2 tablespoons of the oil in a large pot over low heat, add the bacon, and cook for about 2 minutes. Lift the crabs out of their marinade (strain the marinade and set aside) and add to the pot, along with the onion, green onions, parsley, and thyme sprigs and cook for 2 minutes.

Add the tomatoes, cloves, bay leaves, the remaining garlic and chile, and some pepper and a little salt. Add the marinade. Cover and cook over low heat for 10–15 minutes.

(continued)

Add the Colombo powder and the rest of the oil, then add the rice. Mix thoroughly to coat the rice evenly in the sauce. Squeeze in the juice of the remaining lime. Mix gently and add water if necessary to cover the crab and rice by about ⅜ inch (1 cm). Season with salt and pepper, cover, and cook over low heat until the rice is soft, 15–20 minutes, stirring once or twice to ensure the rice doesn't stick to the bottom of the pot and burn. Serve hot.

Suggestion: In my house, we served the matété with a lime wedge on the side to squeeze in while eating. We'd also enjoy it with infused rums such as passion fruit punch (p. 60).

TIP

If you want to upgrade the recipe, make it with lobster tails.

FISH AND SEAFOOD

SALT COD BRANDADE

**This recipe has France written all over it. My parents worked very hard running their
own successful business, so we children all ate at the school canteen. Salt cod brandade
and stewed lentils was my favorite canteen meal. They'd usually serve it on Fridays,
and I really looked forward to it – real comfort food! Serve with stewed lentils (p. 166).**

Serves 4

19 oz (600 g) skinless, boneless dried
   salted cod
3–3½ lb (1.5 kg) true yam
4 tbsp sunflower oil
1 onion, very finely chopped
3 green onions, very finely chopped
3 garlic cloves, very finely chopped
1 sprig thyme, leaves only
2 sprigs parsley, chopped
4 tbsp (2 oz/60 g) butter
1 cup (8 fl oz/250 ml) milk
salt and freshly ground black pepper
2 oz (60 g) Gruyère cheese, grated
2 tbsp fresh or dried bread crumbs

Put the saltfish in a saucepan, add cold water to cover, bring to a boil, and
boil for 5 minutes. Drain off the water and repeat the process. Blend the cod
in a food processor for about 1 minute. Set aside.

Peel the yam and cut into small chunks. Place in a pan of lightly salted boiling
water and boil until completely soft, 30 minutes. Drain and mash with a fork.
Set aside.

Preheat the oven to 400°F (200°C).

Heat the oil in a pot over medium heat, add the onion, green onions, garlic,
thyme, and parsley and cook until softened. Add the cod and stir. Add the
yam, butter, and milk and stir vigorously. Season with salt and pepper. Spread
evenly in a gratin dish and sprinkle the cheese and bread crumbs over the
surface. Bake for about 15 minutes, until the top is golden. Serve hot.

SALTED COD RICE

The first time I had *macadam* was in Martinique. I ate it with my fingers. I remember it because I was struggling to enjoy it fully while keeping the manners my mother insisted on when we ate out. I just went in with my fingers. I'll never forget the look on my mother's face. Hilarious! I guess, subconsciously, I went back to the roots of eating *tiep bou dien*, a Senegalese rice dish made with fish and vegetables that is best enjoyed with your fingers.

Serves 4–6

2 lb (1 kg) skinless, boneless dried
    salted cod
2 tbsp sunflower oil
1 onion, chopped
6 tbsp (2 oz/50 g) coarse cassava flour
    (gari) or coarse cornmeal, similar
    to polenta
8 oz (250 g) tomatoes, chopped
2 cups (16 fl oz/500 ml) hot water
1 bay leaf
1 Scotch bonnet chile
1 sprig thyme
2 green onions, chopped
2 garlic cloves, crushed
2½ cups (1 lb/500 g) long-grain rice
juice of 1 lime
1 sprig parsley, finely chopped

Put the saltfish in a saucepan, add cold water to cover, bring to a boil, and boil for 5 minutes. Discard the water.

Heat the oil in a pot over medium heat, add the onion, and cook until translucent. Add the flour, tomatoes, hot water, bay leaf, the whole chile, thyme sprig, and the green onions. When it comes to a boil, add the fish and garlic and cook over low heat for 30 minutes, stirring occasionally, taking care not to burst the chile.

Meanwhile, boil the rice until tender; drain.

Remove the chile from the fish pot. Add the rice and stir well. Add the lime juice and chopped parsley. Serve hot.

CREOLE FRIED FISH

What I love the most about this dish are the fried onions and chile we traditionally put on top of it. This recipe works best with snapper.

Serves 4

4 small red snapper, scaled and
   cleaned
salt and freshly ground black pepper
2 garlic cloves, very finely chopped
juice of 1 lime, plus lime wedges,
   for serving
2 Scotch bonnet chiles: 1 chopped,
   1 sliced (optional)
about 2½ cups (20 fl oz/600 ml)
   vegetable oil
⅞ cup (4 oz/100 g) all-purpose flour
1 tsp ground allspice
1 onion, thinly sliced

Marinate the fish in the refrigerator overnight with salt and pepper, the garlic, lime juice, chopped chile, and 2 tablespoons of the oil.

Remove the fish from its marinade and pat dry with paper towels.

Put the flour on a large plate and mix with the allspice, salt, and pepper. Roll each fish in the flour.

Heat about 2 cups (16 fl oz/500 ml) of the oil in a large frying pan over medium heat. Add the fish and cook until golden and crisp. Drain on paper towels.

In a saucepan, heat the remaining 6 tablespoons oil and fry the onion until softened, together with the sliced chile, if you're brave.

To serve, put a whole fish on each plate and cover with the fried onions. Serve with lime wedges on the side.

VIANN' É POUL'

MEAT AND POULTRY

◆◆◆◆◆◆◆◆◆◆

Many of these meat dishes are authentic recipes you could try only if they were cooked for you by a local. They are often not sexy on the plate but are definitely what I would call Creole soul food: one-pot, slow-cooked stews that reveal their African heritage.

Cooking meat Creole style means it's what Europeans would consider overcooked. But in the tropical climate, it is necessary to cook meats thoroughly to avoid.food poisoning. It's stewed for hours, until it falls off the bones or melts in your mouth.

I remember the first time I was allowed to make a meat stew for the family Sunday lunch—big responsibility! I was about thirteen years old and had decided to make a rabbit ragout. I'd seen my father make so many of these traditional one-pot stews that I instinctively knew what to do, so I was happy to get on with it, and my dad was pretty proud.

CREOLE PORK RAGOUT

This is the cornerstone of the Creole Christmas dinner. This is why the pig was fed every day throughout the year on breadfruit, nice bananas, and good guavas, so its meat would be juicy and flavorsome. This is why you spend hours marinating the meat and slow-cooking it. It has to be tender, melt in your mouth, and give instant comfort. Serve with stewed pigeon peas (p. 169) and rice or a vegetable gratin.

Serves 4

1½ lb (700 g) pork shoulder,
    cut into chunks
juice of 2 limes
4 garlic cloves, very finely chopped
2 tsp ground allspice
salt and freshly ground black pepper
2 tbsp vegetable oil
2 onions, sliced
2 green onions, chopped
2 sprigs thyme
2 bay leaves
1 clove
1 Scotch bonnet chile
½ cup (4 fl oz/125 ml) water

Marinate the pork in the refrigerator overnight with the juice of 1 lime, half the garlic, half the allspice, and salt and pepper.

Remove the pork from the marinade and pat dry with paper towels. Heat the oil in a large, heavy pot over medium-high heat, add the pork, and cook until browned. Add the onions, green onions, remaining allspice, and salt and pepper and stir and brown for a few minutes.

Add the juice of 1 lime, the remaining garlic, thyme sprigs, bay leaves, clove, the whole chile, and the water. Cover and cook over very low heat for 2 hours, until the meat is very tender.

MIGAN DE FRUIT À PAIN

BREADFRUIT HOT POT

This is an African slave recipe, a simple one-pot stew that truly represents the African heritage in Creole food.

Serves 6

3 salted pigs' tails
1 breadfruit
4 tbsp vegetable oil
7 oz (200 g) salted beef or corned
   beef, diced
3½-oz (100-g) slab smoked bacon,
   diced
about 4 oz (100 g) calabaza
   (West Indian pumpkin) or butternut
   squash, peeled and cubed
1 onion, chopped
4 green onions, chopped
4 garlic cloves, chopped
2 sprigs thyme
1 aji dulce chile, chopped
5 cups (40 fl oz/1.2 liters) water
1 bay leaf
1 clove
2 sprigs parsley, chopped
salt and freshly ground black pepper
1 habanero chile

Clean the pigs' tails in cold water, then put them in a saucepan, add cold water to cover, bring to a boil, and boil for 20 minutes.

Quarter the breadfruit. Peel, remove and discard the core, and cut into cubes.

Drain the pigs' tails and cut into pieces through the joints. Pat dry with paper towels.

Heat the oil in a large pot over medium heat, add the pigs' tails, beef, and bacon, and brown for 2–3 minutes.

Add the breadfruit, calabaza, onion and green onions, garlic, thyme, aji dulce chile, and ½ cup (4 fl oz/125 ml) of the water. Stir, then add the remaining water, the bay leaf, clove, parsley, salt and pepper, and the whole habanero chile. Cover the pot and simmer over low heat for 30–40 minutes, stirring occasionally, taking care not to burst the chile.

Remove the chile. Serve hot.

TIP

Salted pigs' tails are a typical
Caribbean ingredient;
look for them in Afro-
Caribbean shops and online.

COLOMBO DE CABRI

MUTTON COLOMBO

Like most other islands in the Caribbean, Guadeloupe and Martinique have a traditional curry. Ours is called Colombo. We inherited it from the indentured Indians who arrived to work on the islands after slavery was abolished. It is named after the capital city of Sri Lanka and the same name is used for the particular mix of spices we use for this curry; it's easy to make your own (p. 41), but in Guadeloupe and Martinique you will find Colombo in every market stall, in every supermarket, in every household's cupboards, and on every menu. We make Colombo with chicken, pork, mutton, goat, prawns, shark, and even skate. I would go as far as saying it's one of the official dishes of Guadeloupe and Martinique.

Serves 4

2 lb (1 kg) mutton or goat, cut
  into chunks
3 garlic cloves, crushed and very
  finely chopped
6 tbsp Colombo powder (p. 41)
salt and freshly ground black pepper
juice of 1 lime
3 tbsp vegetable oil
2 onions, very finely chopped
3 green onions, chopped
1 tsp tamarind paste
¼ cup (2 fl oz/60 ml) water
1 eggplant, diced
1 sweet potato, diced
4 oz (100 g) true yam, diced
1 Scotch bonnet chile
2 sprigs thyme
2 sprigs parsley, chopped
boiled white basmati or coconut rice
  (p. 154), for serving

Marinate the meat with 1 garlic clove, 2 tablespoons Colombo powder, salt and pepper, the juice of 1 lime, and 1 tablespoon oil for at least 2 hours, or preferably overnight.

Remove the meat from the marinade and pat dry with paper towels. Heat the remaining 2 tablespoons oil in a large, heavy pot over medium-high heat, add the meat, and cook, stirring occasionally, until browned.

Add the onions, green onions, the remaining garlic, the tamarind paste, the remaining Colombo powder, the water, the eggplant, sweet potato, yam, the whole chile, thyme, parsley, and salt and pepper. Reduce the heat, cover the pot, and cook over low heat until the meat is very tender, 45 minutes.

Serve hot, with rice.

BÉBÉLÉ

I love bébélé – tripe with green bananas and dombrés. It's a slave dish, and the name is thought to derive from a Bantu word meaning "small pieces of meat." It's a speciality of Marie-Galante, my mother's island, and is usually served at christenings, first communions, and weddings. It's a very traditional recipe, and fussy locals say they won't eat it from just anyone. If it doesn't look right, they will leave it – and that's not a good sign at a party.

Serves 4–6

1½ lb (700 g) raw tripe, prepared (p. 37, and see Tip)
3 salted pigs' tails
3 tablespoons vegetable oil
2 onions, finely chopped
9 green onions, finely chopped
2 bay leaves
6 cloves
2 carrots, peeled and diced
10 oz (300 g) true yam, peeled and diced
2 malangas (eddo) or dasheen (taro), peeled and diced
½ breadfruit, peeled and diced
7 oz (200 g) calabaza (West Indian pumpkin) or butternut squash, peeled and diced
3 green bananas, peeled and diced
2 oz (50 g) canned green pigeon peas, drained
12-oz (350-g) slab smoked bacon, diced
3 sprigs parsley, chopped
2 sprigs thyme
3 garlic cloves, crushed
salt and freshly ground black pepper
1 habanero chile
Dombré dough, rolled into very small balls (p. 41)

TIP

Outside the Caribbean, tripe is often sold precooked and cleaned, but for this recipe, you need to start with raw tripe. Ask your butcher for advice.

Starting the day before you want to make this dish, prepare the tripe.

Clean the pigs' tails in cold water, then put them in a saucepan, add cold water to cover, bring to a boil, and boil for 20 minutes. Drain and cut the pigs' tails into pieces through the joints.

Heat 2 tablespoons of the oil in a pot, add the onions and 6 green onions, and cook for 2–3 minutes. Add the tripe and tails, stir, and add cold water to cover. Add 1 bay leaf and 1 clove. Cover and simmer gently over medium-low heat until the tripe is meltingly tender, at least 1½ hours. Alternatively, cook for 30 minutes in a pressure cooker over medium heat.

Heat the remaining oil in a large pot over medium heat, add the carrots, and cook for 2–3 minutes. Add all the remaining vegetables, the fruits, and pigeon peas and stir well. Add the cooked tripe and pigs' tails, bacon, parsley, thyme, garlic, and the remaining green onions, bay leaf, and cloves. Season with salt and pepper and add the whole chile. Reduce the heat, add cold water to cover, put the lid on the pot, and cook for 30 minutes over low heat.

Add the dombrés and stir carefully so as not to break up the chile. Add a little boiling water if necessary to cover the dombrés, and cook until the sauce is thick, 20 minutes.

Taste and add more salt if necessary. Remove the chile. Serve hot.

The raw flesh of dasheen can make your hands itch, while green bananas will stain. Before preparing them, oil your hands or wear rubber gloves.

CHICKEN FRICASSÉE

This is a go-to recipe. It's easy to make, with simple ingredients, and it requires minimal attention. Sometimes I replace the whole chicken with chicken legs and slow-cook for an additional 30 minutes until the meat falls off the bone. I then shred the meat and use it to stuff a bokit, instead of corned beef (p. 100). Once the bokit is cooked, I slice it open and add a slice of tomato and some iceberg lettuce – and that's it, a chicken bokit.

Serves 4

1 whole chicken, cut into eight pieces
3 tbsp sunflower oil
juice of 2 limes
3 sprigs thyme
3 garlic cloves, crushed
1 tsp ground allspice
1 tsp pumpkin pie spice
salt and freshly ground black pepper
1 onion, chopped
2 green onions, chopped
2 bay leaves
1 Maggi or bouillon cube, crumbled
1 tbsp raw sugar
¾ cup (6 fl oz/180 ml) water
1 Scotch bonnet chile
boiled rice, for serving
stewed red kidney beans (p. 168),
    for serving

Marinate the chicken in the refrigerator overnight with 1 tablespoon of the oil, the lime juice, thyme, 1 garlic clove, allspice, pumpkin pie spice, and salt and pepper.

Remove the chicken from the marinade (reserve the marinade) and pat dry with paper towels. Heat the remaining 2 tablespoons oil in a large, heavy pot over medium-high heat, add the chicken, and cook, turning occasionally, until golden brown all over.

Add the onion, green onions, and the remaining garlic and cook until lightly browned, 2–3 minutes.

Add the reserved marinade, bay leaves, stock cube, and sugar, then add ½ cup (4 fl oz/120 ml) water and the whole chile, cover, and cook over low heat for 50 minutes.

Add another ¼ cup water (2 fl oz/60 ml) and salt and pepper to taste. Stir, taking care not to burst the chile, cover, and cook for another 15 minutes.

Remove the chile. Serve with boiled rice and stewed beans.

DOMBRÉS, PIGS' TAILS, AND KIDNEY BEANS

This is supposedly a poor man's meal – that's all I ever heard about this dish. A legacy of slavery, it makes the most of pigs' tails, which no one else wanted, slow-cooked in a pot. It has now become an everyday classic. It's what the Italians call "ugly but good"... so filling and soul-nurturing.

Serves 4–6

1 lb (500 g) dried red kidney beans
6 salted pigs' tails
4 tbsp vegetable oil
2 onions, chopped
3 garlic cloves, crushed
5½-oz (150-g) slab smoked bacon, diced
2 green onions, chopped
1 bay leaf
2 sprigs thyme
2 cloves
1½ quarts (48 fl oz/1.5 liters) water
Dombré dough, rolled into small balls (p. 41)
1 tsp ground allspice
salt and freshly ground black pepper
1 habanero chile

Soak the beans in cold water overnight.

Clean the pigs' tails in cold water, then put them in a saucepan, add cold water to cover, bring to a boil, and boil for 20 minutes. Drain and cut the pigs' tails into pieces through the joints.

Heat the oil in a large pot over medium heat, add the onions and garlic, and cook until softened.

Drain and rinse the beans and add them to the pot. Add the pigs' tails, bacon, green onions, bay leaf, thyme, and cloves and cook for 5 minutes. Add the water, put the lid on the pot, and simmer for 1½ hours.

Add the dombrés, allspice, salt, pepper, and the whole chile. Cook until the sauce is thick, 20–25 minutes.

Remove the chile. Serve hot.

TIP

You can use canned red kidney beans: cook the tails, bacon, and flavorings for 1 hour before adding the beans.

CREOLE CASSOULET

This recipe is a Creole version of the famous French cassoulet. It's slow-cooked; it's deliciously sweet from the carrots, with heaps of different flavors. It's not sexy on the plate, but guests never fail to ask for more. It's a crowd-pleaser, especially if you don't explain in detail what the ingredients are before you start eating. (Of course you'd say it's pork, but just not which part.) My most popular recipe yet!

Serves 4–6

2 salted pigs' tails
8 oz (250 g) boneless pork loin, cut into slices 1 inch (2.5 cm) thick
4 tbsp sunflower oil
5½-oz (150-g) slab smoked bacon, diced
1 can or vacuum pack (about 12 oz/ 350 g) cocktail frankfurters, drained
2 onions, chopped
4 garlic cloves, chopped
two 14-oz (400-g) cans mixed peas and beans, drained and rinsed
3 sprigs parsley, chopped
2 sprigs thyme
3 carrots, sliced 1 inch (2.5 cm) thick
1 can or tube (7 oz/200 g) tomato paste
1 Scotch bonnet chile
salt and freshly ground black pepper

Clean the pigs' tails in cold water, then put them in a saucepan, add cold water to cover, bring to a boil, and boil for 20 minutes. Drain the pigs' tails and cut into pieces through the joints. Set aside. Cut each slice of pork loin into three pieces.

Heat half the oil in a frying pan over medium-high heat. Add the pork, bacon, and frankfurters and brown all over. Set aside.

Heat the remaining oil in an ovenproof pot over medium heat, add the onions and garlic, and cook for 3–4 minutes. Add the mixed peas and beans. Add cold water to cover and add the parsley, thyme, carrots, tomato paste, the whole chile, and salt and pepper. Bring to the simmering point, then cover with a well-fitting lid and simmer for 1½ hours, checking the level of water regularly and topping up if necessary to ensure it doesn't dry out.

Add all the meat and simmer for another 1½ hours.

Preheat the oven to 400°F (200°C). Taste the cassoulet and adjust the seasoning if necessary. Put the pot in the oven for 1 hour. Serve hot.

BLAFF DE SALAISONS

SALTED MEAT BLAFF

Whenever there's cured meat, we Creoles love it! This recipe can be traced back to the time of slavery. It's a very rustic meal that works best in winter. When I was growing up, this is the sort of food my dad cooked on Saturdays while my mum was gardening. Blaff supposedly has roots in Holland: both the word and the cooking style are believed to have been introduced by Dutch traders. When I visited a Dutch village I tasted a broth with salted meat that was very similar to this – it was described as old-style Dutch food.

Serves 4

8 oz (250 g) salted pigs' tails
8 oz (250 g) salted beef or corned beef
8 oz (250 g) salted pig's snout
6 tbsp sunflower oil
juice of 2 limes
1 carrot, roughly chopped
1 parsnip, roughly chopped
2 onions: 1 roughly chopped, 1 very finely chopped
4 green onions, chopped
6 garlic cloves: 3 crushed, 3 very finely chopped
½ green cabbage, roughly chopped
1 Maggi or bouillon cube
1 tsp ground allspice
ground black pepper
½ cup (4 fl oz/125 ml) water
3 sprigs parsley, chopped
½ Scotch bonnet chile, very finely chopped
2 sprigs thyme, leaves only

Chop the pigs' tails through the joints, slice the salted beef, and chop the snout into cubes. Put all the meats in a large saucepan, add cold water to cover, bring to a boil, and then simmer for about 30 minutes in order to desalt and soften the meats. Drain and set aside.

Heat 2 tablespoons of the oil in a large pot over medium-high heat and brown the meats. Add the juice of 1 lime and stir to deglaze the pot, then add the carrot, parsnip, roughly chopped onion, green onions, 3 crushed garlic cloves, and the cabbage and cook until browned.

Add the Maggi cube, allspice, pepper, and the water. Cover the pot and cook over low heat until the meat is very tender, about 2 hours.

Meanwhile, heat 2 tablespoons of the oil in a frying pan over medium heat and add the finely chopped onion, chopped garlic, parsley, chile, and the juice of 1 lime. Cook for 2 minutes, then add the thyme and 2 remaining tablespoons oil. Mix evenly and set aside.

When ready to serve, reheat the onion mixture and spoon over the meat.

OCTOPUS CHICKEN

The original recipe is for chicken and conch, but living in the UK, I find conch is virtually impossible to get unless you smuggle it in from France. I love octopus, so I've adapted the recipe. A Creole-style "surf and turf," which I enjoy with boiled basmati rice.

Serves 4

1 large chicken, cut into eight pieces
juice of 2 limes
3 garlic cloves, crushed
salt and freshly ground black pepper
4 tbsp vegetable oil
1½ onions, very finely chopped
2 sprigs thyme
1 pinch ground allspice
4 sprigs parsley, finely chopped
6 tbsp (3 fl oz/100 ml) water
2 bay leaves
1 Scotch bonnet chile
1 lb (500 g) octopus, gutted, cleaned, and beak removed
2 green onions, very finely chopped
2 tomatoes, chopped
2 heaping tbsp tomato paste

Marinate the chicken with the juice of 1 lime, 1 garlic clove, salt, and pepper for at least 2 hours.

Remove the chicken from the marinade (discard the marinade) and pat dry with paper towels. Heat half the oil in a large, heavy pot over medium-high heat, add the chicken, and cook for about 5 minutes, turning the pieces until golden brown all over.

Add 1 onion, 1 garlic clove, 1 thyme sprig, the allspice, and half the parsley and cook for 2 minutes. Add the water, bay leaves, the whole chile, and salt and pepper and cook over medium-low heat for 20 minutes.

Wash the octopus at least twice under fresh water and then clean it by rubbing it all over with the juice of 1 lime. Wrap the octopus in plastic wrap and pound it with a mallet or a rolling pin (or the bottom of a heavy saucepan) for about 5 minutes.

Cut the octopus into small pieces. Heat the remaining oil in a saucepan over medium heat and sauté the octopus with the green onions, the remaining onion, garlic, thyme, and parsley, the tomatoes, and the tomato paste for 8–10 minutes. Add salt and pepper to taste, then add the octopus to the chicken.

If you are using an ovenproof pot, preheat the oven to 350°F (180°C) and bake for 15–20 minutes. Alternatively, cover the pot with a well-fitting lid and simmer over low heat for 35 minutes. Serve hot.

AILES DE DINDE BOUCANÉES

BUCCANEER TURKEY WINGS

Roadside food at its best. Buccaneer chicken is the most widespread version, but the same technique is applied to turkey wings and spare ribs. When you were on the way to the beach, this is the type of food you'd pick up and enjoy with Creole rice (p. 152) with your feet in the sand and some *sauce chien* or hot Creole sauce on the side (p. 190). When we stop, everybody knows what I want: get me three turkey wings with a lot of sauce and I'm happy!

Serves 4

4 turkey wings
1 habanero chile, very finely chopped
juice of 4 limes
1 tbsp sunflower oil
1 tbsp white vinegar
1 pinch ground cloves
salt and freshly ground black pepper
1 piece of sugarcane (with its skin on),
　about 3 feet (90 cm) long, cut
　into two or three pieces to fit
　the barbecue

Make two cuts on each wing and marinate them in the refrigerator overnight with the chile, lime juice, oil, vinegar, cloves, and salt and pepper.

Light your barbecue charcoal and wait until the embers are white-hot. Put the sugarcane on the barbecue; it will produce thick smoke. Place the wings right where the smoke is thickest and cover the wings with foil or a stainless steel bowl. Grill over direct heat for 45–50 minutes.

Alternatively, if you can't barbecue, cook the wings in a preheated oven at 425°F (220°C) for 45–50 minutes; they won't have the smoky flavor, but the marinade will do the trick.

TIP

If you're not a turkey person,
replace with a whole chicken,
cut into four pieces.

GIGOT DE PÂQUES

EASTER SUNDAY LAMB

Just as in France, Creoles like to have lamb for Easter Sunday. It's usually served with yam gratin (p. 162), and it needs to be cooked until well done.

Serves 6

3–3½ lb (1.5 kg) leg of lamb
salt and freshly ground black pepper
3 tbsp sunflower oil
juice of 2 limes
1 Scotch bonnet chile, chopped
1 onion, chopped
3 green onions, chopped
6 sprigs thyme
2 tbsp Colombo powder (p. 41)
1 tsp ground allspice
1 tsp pumpkin pie spice
8 garlic cloves, quartered
6 cloves, halved
⅔ cup (5 fl oz/150 ml) water

You will need to marinate the lamb for at least 4 hours or overnight. Put the lamb in a large bowl or container with a lid: it must be big enough to contain the lamb and small enough to fit in the refrigerator. Rub the leg with salt, pepper, 1 tablespoon of the oil, and the lime juice. Wearing rubber gloves, rub the leg all over with the chopped chile, onion, green onions, and thyme. Sprinkle the Colombo powder, allspice, and pumpkin pie spice all over the lamb. Using a small sharp knife, stab the leg all over and insert the pieces of garlic and the cloves into the holes. Drizzle with another tablespoon of oil, cover, and leave to marinate in the refrigerator.

Preheat the oven to 400°F (200°C).

Put the lamb in a roasting pan, reserving the marinade. Drizzle the remaining oil over the lamb. Put the lamb in the oven. Every 15 minutes, turn the lamb to ensure it cooks evenly; stir the jus in the roasting pan and spoon it over the leg every time you turn it. After about 40 minutes, remove the lamb from the oven, baste with the reserved marinade, and add the water to the pan. Return to the oven and cook for another 35–40 minutes (about 75 minutes total).

When the lamb is cooked to your liking (see Tip), remove from the oven, cover with foil, and leave to rest for 10–15 minutes before carving and serving.

Strain the sauce through a fine sieve and, if necessary, boil to reduce and thicken slightly before serving with the lamb.

TIP

In Creole food, meat is very well cooked. If you like your lamb a bit pink, cook it for 60 minutes, but use a meat thermometer to check the internal temperature, which should be 130°–140°F (55°–60°C).

MEAT AND POULTRY

BREADFRUIT AND PORK PARMENTIER

Tout est bon dans le cochon ("in the pig, everything is good") is more than just a French saying. During the Christmas season, when someone in the neighborhood kills a pig, you can be sure all of it will be used. It's almost like paying tribute to the animal to use it fully. You can order the bits of the animal you want from your neighbor before the animal is killed. This is one way to use the pork.

Serves 4

2 lb (1 kg) boneless pork shoulder
salt and freshly ground black pepper
½ tsp pumpkin pie spice
½ tsp ground allspice
1 tbsp Colombo powder (p. 41)
6 garlic cloves, crushed
1 Scotch bonnet chile, finely chopped
2 onions, very finely chopped
2 Maggi or bouillon cubes, dissolved
    in 1¼ cups (10 fl oz/300 ml)
    boiling water
1 breadfruit
3 tbsp butter, plus extra
    for topping
⅞ cup (7 fl oz/200 ml) milk
1 tbsp crème fraîche
4 oz (100 g) Emmentaler cheese,
    grated

TIP

You can reserve the sauce and
use it to cook vegetables.

Preheat the oven to 350°F (180°C).

Cut off any excess fat from the shoulder. Sprinkle the pork with salt, pepper, pumpkin pie spice, allspice, and Colombo powder and rub them in. Using a small sharp knife, pierce the shoulder all over and push the garlic and chile into the holes.

Put the pork in an ovenproof pot. Add the onions. Pour the Maggi stock over the pork: it should come about halfway up the pork. Cover the pot with a well-fitting lid and place it in the oven for about 2 hours.

Peel the breadfruit, cut into quarters, and cut out the core. Place in a pan of lightly salted boiling water and boil for 40 minutes. Drain the water and mash with a fork. Add the butter, milk, and crème fraîche. Mix well, taste, and add more salt if necessary.

Check the pork: if it is fork tender and falling apart, remove it from the oven. If not, cook it for another 30 minutes.

Remove the pot from the oven, take the pork out of the sauce, and place in a large dish. Shred the meat with a fork and knife.

Spread half of the breadfruit purée in a large gratin dish. Cover with the pork and then with the rest of the purée. Sprinkle the cheese and a few knobs of butter over the surface and bake in the oven for 15 minutes, until the top is golden. Serve hot.

RAGOUT DE BOEUF

CREOLE BEEF POT ROAST

The best beef ragout I ever had was at my friend's grandmother's house. It cooked for hours in her tiny, very simple kitchen. It was salty, the cuts of beef were fatty with some bones, and the seasoning was to die for. She has since passed away, but from my delicious memories I have been able to replicate the recipe. Serve with Creole rice (p. 152).

Serves 4

3–3½ lb (1.5 kg) stewing beef with
    bones and fat
5 garlic cloves: 2 crushed,
    3 very finely chopped
2 sprigs thyme
4 tbsp vegetable oil
juice of 1 lime
salt and freshly ground black pepper
2 onions, very finely chopped
1 tbsp ground allspice
1 tbsp pumpkin pie spice
2 bay leaves
1 tbsp white vinegar
1 Maggi or bouillon cube
1 carrot, diced
1 Caribbean red habanero chile

Marinate the meat in the refrigerator overnight with the crushed garlic, 1 sprig of thyme, 1 tablespoon oil, the lime juice, and salt and pepper.

Remove the meat from the marinade and pat dry with paper towels. Heat the remaining oil in a large, heavy pot over medium-high heat, add the meat, and brown well all over.

Add the onions and the chopped garlic and cook over medium heat until softened. Add the remaining thyme, the allspice, pumpkin pie spice, bay leaves, and the vinegar and stir. Add just enough hot water to cover the meat and add the Maggi cube, salt and pepper, the carrot and the whole chile. Cover and cook over very low heat for at least 2 hours.

Stir carefully to avoid breaking up the chile. The meat should be very tender; if not, cover and simmer for another 10–15 minutes. You may need to add a tiny bit more hot water.

Taste and adjust the seasoning and remove the chile. Serve hot.

AKONPAYMAN

SIDES

Creole food is all about feasting and indulging. If you stay
true to its roots, you will find rich, delicious recipes that feed
not only your body but also your soul. Sides are sometimes
as rich as mains. A Creole plate is a full plate, and if you eat
in a Creole household, you'd better not disappoint the
cook by eating like a bird. We want to feed you and
leave you with a full tummy. That's the Creole way!

CREOLE RICE

Creole rice (also called *riz melangé*) is a housewife's godsend. When she serves this rice — to which you can add chicken or fish — it means she was either in a rush or just used whatever was in her cupboard. It's also a favorite to bring when spending a day on the beach with the family and barbecuing some chicken wings in situ. Try it with chicken fricassée (p. 138).

Serves 4

2 eggs
2 tbsp vegetable oil
1 onion, very finely chopped
1 green onion, very finely chopped
4 garlic cloves, very finely chopped
½ tsp Colombo powder (p. 41)
½ tsp tomato paste
2½ cups (1 lb/500 g) jasmine rice
1 can (about 10 oz/300 g) corn
  kernels, drained
2 cups (16 fl oz/500 ml) water
2 Maggi or bouillon cubes
1 bay leaf
salt and freshly ground black pepper

Put the eggs in a saucepan of cold water, bring to simmering point, and simmer for 7–10 minutes. Drain and rinse in cold water. Set aside.

Heat the oil in a large saucepan, add the onion, green onion, garlic, Colombo powder, and tomato paste and cook until the onions start to soften.

Add the rice and corn. Stir to coat the rice. Add the water, chicken cubes, and bay leaf and stir well. Add salt and pepper. Cover and cook over low heat for 25 minutes, stirring two or three times to ensure the rice doesn't stick to the bottom of the pan.

Cut each egg into sixths and stir into the rice. Remove the bay leaf and serve hot.

OKRA RICE

Okra was brought to the Caribbean on the slave boats. You'll find a similar recipe in African cuisine. It looks fabulous on the plate with something as simple as stewed chicken. Okra is easy to find nowadays in most supermarkets.

Serves 4

8 oz (250 g) fresh okra
1 quart (32 fl oz/1 liter) water
1 onion, very finely chopped
4 garlic cloves, very finely chopped
1 bay leaf
1 tbsp vegetable oil
salt and freshly ground black pepper
⅞ cup (7 fl oz/200 ml) coconut milk
generous 3 cups (19 oz/600 g)
   basmati rice

Slice the okra into rings ⅜ inch (1 cm) thick. Put them in a pot and add the water, onion, garlic, bay leaf, oil, and salt and pepper. Bring to the simmering point, then add the coconut milk and simmer for about 2 minutes.

Meanwhile, rinse the rice three times. Drain and add the rice to the pot. Cover and cook over low heat for about 25 minutes; stir after 10–12 minutes to ensure the okra is evenly distributed in the rice and the rice is not sticking to the bottom of the pot. When the rice is tender and has absorbed most of the liquid, but is still quite wet, it is ready to serve.

RIZ AU COCO

COCONUT RICE

A classic alternative to plain white rice. The taste of the coconut isn't overpowering, and this works well with a good old Colombo curry.

Serves 4

2½ cups (1 lb/500 g) basmati rice
1⅓ cups (13 fl oz/400 ml)
   coconut milk
3 tbsp water
salt
1 tbsp vegetable oil

Wash the rice in a mixing bowl at least three times, until the water is clear. Drain and put the rice in a saucepan. Add the coconut milk, water, salt, and oil. Cover and cook over low heat for 25 minutes; stir after 10–12 minutes to keep the rice from sticking to the bottom of the pan. Serve hot.

CINDY'S PLANTAIN GRATIN

My sister likes everything fried. She's greedy. Whatever you cook for her, if there's not butter or frying involved, she'll quickly go and fix it. I created this recipe for her because she loves bacon, and it's a pleasure to see her face when she enjoys food. Makes my day!

Serves 4

2 plantains
4 tbsp sunflower oil
1 handful smoked bacon lardons
2 tbsp butter
⅓ cup (1½ oz/45 g) all-purpose flour
2 cups (16 fl oz/500 ml) milk
salt and freshly ground black pepper
1 pinch grated nutmeg
4 oz (100 g) Emmentaler cheese, grated

Preheat the oven to 400°F (200°C).

Peel the plantains and slice them about ¾ inch (2 cm) thick.

Heat the oil in a frying pan and fry the lardons until crisp. Add the plantains and cook for 2–3 minutes. Tip them into a gratin dish.

Make a béchamel sauce: melt the butter in a saucepan over medium heat, add the flour, and whisk thoroughly. Gradually add the milk, whisking until it thickens, then stir in salt, pepper, nutmeg, and 3 tablespoons of the cheese.

Pour the béchamel over the plantains and sprinkle the remaining cheese over the top. Bake for 15 minutes, until golden. Serve hot.

GRATIN DE BANANES JAUNES DE MAMOUNE

MAMOUNE'S PLANTAIN GRATIN

My mother was the master of gratins, effortlessly whipping up these things to go with our Sunday lunch. She cooks Creole food faster than anyone else I've seen. She loves a good rich béchamel, with loads of cheese, so this dish is for her.

Serves 4

3 plantains
salt and freshly ground black pepper
2 tbsp butter
⅓ cup (1½ oz/45 g) all-purpose flour
2 cups (16 fl oz/500 ml) milk
1 pinch grated nutmeg
7 oz (200 g) Emmentaler cheese, grated

Preheat the oven to 400°F (200°C).

Chop off the ends of the plantains and cut the plantains in half. Place them in a pan of boiling water, add 2 pinches of salt, and boil for 10 minutes. Drain the plantains and remove the skin, which should fall off quite easily. Slice the plantains about 1 inch (2.5 cm) thick.

Make a béchamel sauce: melt the butter in a saucepan over medium heat, add the flour, and whisk thoroughly. Gradually add the milk, whisking until it thickens, then stir in salt, pepper, nutmeg, and 6 tablespoons (50 g) of the cheese.

Put a layer of plantains in a gratin dish, sprinkle some cheese over them, then add a layer of béchamel sauce. Repeat the layers. Sprinkle the remaining cheese over the top. Bake until golden, 15 minutes. Serve hot.

LIGHT PLANTAIN GRATIN

This is how I make a plantain gratin at home. It's a lighter version than some other gratins because I don't use béchamel sauce. So easy to do after a long day of work.

Serves 4

4 plantains
salt and freshly ground black pepper
⅞ cup (7 fl oz/200 ml) crème fraîche
2–3 knobs of butter
1 pinch grated cinnamon
4 oz (100 g) Emmentaler cheese,
   grated

Preheat the oven to 400°F (200°C).

Chop off the ends of the plantains and cut the plantains in half. Place them in a pan of boiling water, add 2 pinches of salt, and boil for 10 minutes. Drain the plantains and remove the skins. Slice two of the plantains about 1 inch (2.5 cm) thick.

Blend the remaining plantains in a food processor. Add the crème fraîche and butter and blend to a smooth purée. Season with salt, pepper, and cinnamon to taste.

Put a layer of plantain slices in a gratin dish and cover with a layer of the purée. Repeat the layers. Sprinkle the cheese over the top. Bake until golden, 15 minutes. Serve hot.

GREEN BANANA CAKES

This is very close to what Haitians call banana *pézé*. I created this recipe in London after trying my friend's speciality; her mother is from Haiti. There's a massive Haitian community in Guadeloupe, primarily because extreme poverty drives many to migrate to find work, and if they stay long enough they have a chance to obtain French nationality, social security, and education for their family. It adds to the fusion and is what makes the Caribbean so beautiful. I love green bananas because of their dryness and simplicity. This is my humble take on the Haitian dish.

Serves 4

3 tbsp vegetable oil, plus extra for
  your hands
1½ lb (750 g) green bananas
4 garlic cloves, finely grated
1 green onion,
  very finely chopped
1 egg, beaten
2½ tbsp all-purpose flour
salt and freshly ground black pepper

Coat your hands in oil to prevent the bananas from staining them. Peel the bananas, then coarsely grate them into a mixing bowl.

Add the garlic and green onion, mix them together, and then stir in the egg. Add the flour and stir to combine thoroughly, then season with salt and pepper.

Heat the oil in a frying pan over medium heat. Drop 3–5 tablespoonfuls of the mixture into the frying pan and flatten them, then fry, turning once, until golden on both sides. Drain on paper towels. Repeat until you have used all the mixture. Serve hot.

YAM GRATIN

If you're having Easter lamb roast in Guadeloupe or Martinique, nine times out of ten it will be served with yam gratin. It's just one of those things. Try this one and serve it with lamb.

Serves 4–6

2 lb (1 kg) true yam
salt and freshly ground black pepper
2 tbsp sunflower oil
1 onion, very finely chopped
1 green onion,
   very finely chopped
2 sprigs parsley, very finely chopped
1 tbsp cornstarch
1½ cups (12 fl oz/350 ml) milk
4 oz (100 g) Emmentaler cheese,
   grated

Preheat the oven to 350°F (180°C).

Peel the yam and cut into small chunks. Place in a pan of lightly salted boiling water and boil for 30 minutes, until tender. Drain and mash with a fork. Set aside.

Heat the oil in a saucepan, add the onion, green onion, and parsley, and sauté for 2 minutes. Add the cornstarch and stir, then gradually add the milk, stirring all the time until smooth. Add some pepper and a third of the cheese. Stir into the mashed yam and season with salt and pepper.

Transfer the mash to a gratin dish. Sprinkle the remaining cheese over the top. Bake until golden and patched with brown, 30 minutes. Serve hot.

GRATIN DE PAPAYES VERTES

GREEN PAPAYA GRATIN

This is a classic of Caribbean Creole cuisine. If you can't find green papayas, choose the least ripe of those you find. When ripe, the papayas have a bit of sweetness that will be enjoyable anyway. Serve hot with fricassée of octopus (p. 107) or chicken (p. 138).

Serves 4

3⅓ lb (1.5kg) green papayas
salt and freshly ground black pepper
2 tbsp sunflower oil
3 tbsp butter
2 garlic cloves, finely chopped
3 green onions, sliced
2 tbsp chopped parsley
2 cups (16 fl oz/500 ml) milk
5 oz (150 g) Gruyère cheese, grated,
   plus extra for sprinkling

Preheat the oven to 425°F (220°C).

Peel the papayas, cut in half, and scoop out the seeds. Cook them in salted boiling water for about 20 minutes (10 minutes if using ripe papayas), then drain and mash with a fork.

Heat the oil and butter in a saucepan over medium-low heat. Add the garlic and green onions and cook for 2 minutes. Stir in the parsley. Add the milk, the mashed papaya, and the cheese. Stir and remove from the heat.

Divide this mixture among 4 ramekins. Sprinkle with cheese. Bake until golden, 10 minutes. Serve hot.

FRIED OKRA

This simple classic Caribbean Creole dish was very popular when I was growing up, but the tradition of making it seems to have disappeared. It's an indispensable recipe in the repertoire of any Creole cook. Try it with *sauce chien* (p. 190).

Serves 4

8 oz (250 g) fresh okra
1 egg
1 tbsp coconut milk
1 tbsp ground allspice
1 tbsp Colombo powder (p. 41)
1 tsp hot chile powder
salt and freshly ground black pepper
⅓ cup (2 oz/50 g) all-purpose flour
1 cup (8 fl oz/250 ml) vegetable oil

Wash the okra thoroughly.

Whisk the egg and coconut milk together until completely smooth. Dip the okra in the egg mixture, then place in a mixing bowl. Sprinkle with the allspice, Colombo powder, chile powder, and salt and pepper and toss gently to coat evenly. Add the flour and stir to coat evenly.

Heat the oil in a frying pan over medium heat until it reaches 350°F (180°C) or until a cube of bread browns in 3 seconds. Gently drop the okra into the oil and cook, turning occasionally, until golden and crisp, 4–5 minutes.

Using a slotted spoon, scoop the okra out of the oil and drain on paper towels. Serve hot, with *sauce chien* (p. 190) on the side, if you like.

STEWED LENTILS

Good things come to those who wait. When my dad was making these I remember going back and forth, lifting the lid to check whether they were ready. It takes ages – you can watch a movie while these are simmering – but the flavors are worth it in the end. Serve hot with salted cod *brandade* (p. 123) or with fried fish and rice.

Serves 4

1⅓ cups (8 oz/250 g) green or
    brown lentils
2 tbsp sunflower oil
1 onion, roughly chopped
2 green onions, chopped
3 garlic cloves, roughly crushed
2 cups (16 fl oz/500 ml) hot water
1 salted pig's tail (optional)
7-oz (200-g) slab smoked bacon,
    cut into chunks
1 carrot, diced
2 sprigs thyme
1 clove
1 bay leaf
14 oz (400 g) calabaza (West Indian
    pumpkin) or butternut squash,
    peeled and cubed
salt and freshly ground black pepper
2 sprigs parsley

Soak the lentils overnight in a covered bowl.

Rinse the lentils in two changes of cold water and drain in a colander.

Heat the oil in a pot over medium heat and sauté the onion, green onions, and garlic. Add the lentils and cover with the hot water. Simmer, covered, for 35 minutes.

Meanwhile, if using, clean the pig's tail in cold water, then put it in a saucepan, add cold water to cover, bring to a boil, and boil for 20 minutes. Drain and cut into pieces through the joints.

Add the pig's tail and bacon to the lentils, together with the carrot, thyme, clove, and bay leaf and cook, covered, over medium-low heat for 30 minutes.

Add the calabaza. If the lentils are drying out, add a few tablespoons of water. Taste and adjust the seasoning. Add the parsley, cover, and simmer for another 30 minutes, until thick. Serve hot.

TIP

If using canned lentils, halve all
the lentil cooking times.

STEWED RED KIDNEY BEANS

Almost everyone in Guadeloupe and Martinique has a pressure cooker, which means that this dish can be made in a third of the time. I don't have a pressure cooker in London, so patience is key, as this takes 3 hours of slow cooking. This stew is as traditional as it gets: it's on Creole tables every week, at least on Sundays, without exception. Serve alongside white rice, perhaps with a meat ragout.

Serves 4

2 cups (14 oz/400 g) dried red kidney beans
2 tbsp vegetable oil
1 onion, sliced
2 green onions, sliced
3 garlic cloves, crushed
3¾ cups (30 fl oz/900 ml) hot water
2 sprigs thyme
1 bay leaf
1 clove
7-oz (200-g) slab smoked bacon, roughly chopped
salt and freshly ground black pepper
2 sprigs parsley, chopped

Soak the kidney beans overnight.

Drain the beans and rinse in a colander.

Heat the oil in a large pot over medium heat, add the onion and green onions, and cook until the onions have softened. Add the beans and the garlic. Stir and cover with about 3⅓ cups (27 fl oz/800 ml) of the hot water. Add the thyme, bay leaf, and clove, cover, and simmer over low heat for 1 hour.

Add the bacon and the remaining water and cook, covered, for another hour.

Add salt and pepper to taste and cook for another 30–45 minutes, until the beans are coated in a thick sauce. Stir in the parsley and cook over low heat for another 15 minutes.

TIP

If using canned beans divide all cooking times by three.

IGNAME ET POIS DE BOIS

STEWED GREEN PIGEON PEAS AND YAM

When you cook this, it will smell like a Creole Christmas in your kitchen. It's traditionally served with the Creole pork ragout (p. 130), but it's a festive recipe that can be cooked throughout the year to extend the holiday spirit. Serve at Christmas with pork ragout and boiled yams to follow tradition or with rice and chicken fricassée at any time of year.

Serves 4

2 tbsp vegetable oil
7-oz (200-g) slab smoked bacon, cut into chunks
2 onions, chopped
6 green onions, chopped
14 oz (400 g) calabaza (West Indian pumpkin), peeled and cubed, or 2 carrots, peeled and chopped
3 garlic cloves, crushed
3–4 sprigs parsley, chopped
2–3 sprigs thyme, leaves only
1 lb (500 g) canned green pigeon peas (gungo peas), drained and rinsed
1 tsp ground black pepper
6 cloves
3 bay leaves
1 small piece (7 oz/200 g) true yam (the size of a potato)
salt

Heat the oil in a pot over medium heat and fry the bacon with the onions, green onions, calabaza, garlic, parsley, and thyme for about 5 minutes, stirring, until the bacon is golden brown all over.

Add the pigeon peas and cook for 15 minutes.

Add the pepper, cloves, bay leaves, and the piece of yam. Cover with hot water, add a good pinch of salt, and cook, covered, for 45 minutes.

Remove the lid and cook for an additional 10 minutes to reduce and thicken the liquid.

Using a fork, crush the piece of yam against the wall of the pot. Remove the bay leaf and serve hot.

GIRAUMONADE

CALABAZA MASH

A visit to my coffee-planting friends on the leeward coast of Guadeloupe changed my views on this dish. I had always thought of *giraumonade* as a way of disguising pumpkin, but my friends used a pumpkin they had grown themselves and made it the focus of the dish. They prepared it in the most rural, rustic way, in a basic tin-roofed hut, with an even more basic kitchen with next to no utensils. To this day, it's the best I have ever had.

Serves 4

2 lb (1 kg) calabaza (West Indian
   pumpkin) or butternut squash,
   peeled and cubed
salt and freshly ground black pepper
1 tbsp sunflower oil
4 oz (100 g) smoked bacon,
   cut into lardons
3 green onions, finely chopped
3 garlic cloves, crushed
1 sprig thyme, leaves only
2 sprigs parsley, chopped
1 knob of butter

Put the calabaza in a pan of boiling water with 2 pinches of salt and boil until very tender, 15–20 minutes. Drain and mash with a fork.

Heat the oil in a saucepan, add the lardons, and cook for about 2 minutes. Add the green onions, garlic, thyme, and parsley. Stir in the mashed calabaza and add a knob of butter. Taste and adjust the seasoning. Serve hot.

SMOKED HERRING RICE

I could eat this and nothing else. It's a filling rice dish, but you could never get away with serving just this to a Creole—they'd ask you where the rest of the food is. It's a generous side that will go well with the fish blaff (p. 115), for example.

Serves 4

10 oz (300 g) smoked herring
2 tbsp vegetable oil
1 onion, very finely chopped
1 green onion, very finely chopped
3 garlic cloves, very finely chopped
½ Scotch bonnet chile, very finely
   chopped
2 sprigs parsley, chopped
juice of 1 lime
1 large ripe tomato, cut into
   large cubes
2½ cups (1 lb/500 g) basmati rice

First prepare your herring: slice the belly of the fish open and check if there is an egg pocket; if so, discard it. Clean the fish in cold water, then put it in a saucepan, add cold water to cover, bring to a boil, and boil for 5 minutes.

Drain the herring, reserving the water, and leave to cool. Remove the flesh from the bones, taking care to pick out every single bone. Flake the fish with your fingertips until it is completely shredded.

Heat the oil in a pot and sauté the shredded herring for a minute or two. Add the onion, green onion, garlic, chile, and parsley and cook for 2 minutes. Add the lime juice, stir, and add the tomato.

Meanwhile, rinse the rice three times. Drain and add the rice to the pot and stir to distribute the herring evenly. Add the reserved water from boiling the herring; it should come about 1 inch (2.5 cm) above the rice; if not, top up with boiling water. Cover and cook over low heat for 20 minutes. When the rice has absorbed all the liquid and is tender, but not too soft, it is ready to serve.

RIZ HARICOTS ROUGES

RICE AND BEANS

In Guadeloupe and Martinique, kidney beans are either stewed (p. 168) or cooked with rice, as here. This is a very easy recipe that's seen on every table.

Serves 4

1 cup (7 oz/200 g) dried red kidney
    beans
1½ quarts (48 fl oz/1.5 liters) water
salt and freshly ground black pepper
1 bay leaf
1 clove
1 sprig thyme
7-oz (200-g) slab smoked bacon,
    roughly chopped
1 large onion, chopped
2 garlic cloves, crushed
1½ cups (10 oz/300 g) long-grain rice
3 tbsp sunflower oil
1 sprig parsley, finely chopped

Soak the kidney beans overnight.

Rinse the beans under running water. Put the beans in a pot with the water, a pinch of salt, the bay leaf, clove, and thyme. Cover and cook over medium heat for 2 hours.

Add the bacon, onion, and garlic and cook for 30 minutes.

Meanwhile, rinse the rice three times, drain, and set aside. When the beans are soft, add the rice and enough hot water to cover the rice by about 1 inch (2.5 cm). Add the oil and salt and pepper, cover with the lid, and simmer for 15 minutes, stirring regularly so nothing sticks to the bottom. When the rice is cooked and has absorbed the liquid, but is still moist, it is ready. Sprinkle with the parsley and serve.

SOUP'

SOUPS

◆◆◆◆◆◆◆◆◆

Creole tradition dictates you have soup at least one night
a week. It's very likely to be Sunday night after the feast
enjoyed for lunch. Some soups, such as fat soup,
are the kind we have every week. Others, such as
pâté en pot, are celebration soups. The sweet potato
and ginger soup in this chapter is one I developed
when away from home on cold nights in Europe.

PÂTÉ EN POT

Pâté en pot **is the most poignant reminder of my father; the recipe goes back to his childhood, growing up in the countryside of Martinique. It was the soup of celebrations, christenings, and weddings because it takes so long to make. We had to cut all the ingredients as finely as possible. He would inspect everything and would ask us to cut again, systematically. It had to be perfect! It requires meticulous work to prepare but has such rich, authentic flavors. It's also a recipe that is history-laden: its origin dates back to slavery, and it has elements that are reminiscent of West African soups. It doesn't use the most glorious parts of the animal: we would use the offal from mutton, but beef or lamb offal are fine too. I admit that mudgeon, ruffle, and caul are difficult to find—you need to order them from a knowledgeable butcher—and you can leave them out. If you want a true taste of Creole food from Martinique,** *pâté en pot* **is indisputably** *the* **recipe you must try.**

Serves 6

1 mutton, beef, or lamb heart, about 5 oz (150 g)
14 oz (400 g) tripe
10 oz (300 g) mudgeon, ruffle, or caul (optional)
juice of 3 limes
4 onions: 1 sliced, 3 finely chopped
6 cloves
4 bay leaves
10 garlic cloves: 5 crushed, 5 very finely chopped
salt and freshly ground black pepper
5 tbsp vegetable oil
4 green onions, very finely chopped
6 sprigs thyme
6 sprigs parsley, very finely chopped
3 carrots, very finely diced
2 parsnips, very finely diced
1 leek, very finely chopped
1 rib celery, very finely diced
1 lb (500 g) calabaza (West Indian pumpkin) or butternut squash, very finely diced
2 pieces of true yam (the size of small potatoes), very finely chopped
5½-oz (150-g) slab smoked bacon, very finely diced
2 Maggi cubes or liquid seasoning
1 habanero chile
2 cups (16 fl oz/500 ml) dry white wine
1 small jar (4 oz/100 g) capers, drained

Wash the offal under cold water and clean it thoroughly with the lime juice. Put the offal in a large pot with the sliced onion, 3 cloves, 2 bay leaves, the crushed garlic, and 2 pinches of salt. Add cold water to cover, bring to a boil over low heat, and simmer for 1 hour, skimming regularly to remove the foam that appears on the surface. When the offal is thoroughly cooked, drain, reserving the cooking broth. Cut all the offal into very small cubes. Alternatively, if you can't bear the meticulous work, chop the offal in a food processor until it has a texture similar to coarse ground meat.

Heat the oil in a large pot over medium heat, add the finely chopped onions, the green onions, thyme, parsley, and the remaining cloves and finely chopped garlic. Cook until the onions have softened, 2–3 minutes.

Add the carrots, parsnips, leek, celery, calabaza, and yam. Stir, then add the offal and bacon and stir thoroughly to ensure nothing sticks to the bottom of the pot. Strain the offal broth and pour the broth over the meat and vegetables. Add the Maggi cubes, salt and pepper, and the whole chile. Cover with a lid and cook over low heat for 1½ hours.

Add the wine and capers and cook for 15 minutes. Remove the chile and serve very hot.

CALABAZA AND PRAWN SOUP

In Guadeloupe and Martinique, calabaza grows like a weed. In my garden, they are huge: remember Cinderella's pumpkin coach, and you're getting the picture! One slice easily feeds four; leftover pumpkin freezes well.

Serves 4

1 lb (500 g) calabaza (West Indian pumpkin) or butternut squash, peeled and cubed
salt and freshly ground black pepper
1 onion, finely chopped
2 garlic cloves, crushed
2 sprigs parsley, chopped
8 oz (250 g) raw peeled prawns or jumbo shrimp
1 cup (8 fl oz/250 ml) canned coconut milk
1 pinch grated nutmeg
2 tbsp butter

Put the calabaza in a pan of boiling water with a pinch of salt and pepper, the onion, garlic, parsley, and prawns and boil until the calabaza is tender, 15 minutes.

Pour the contents of the pan into a food processor, add the coconut milk and nutmeg, and blend until smooth, then return the purée to the pan and cook over low heat for 10 minutes.

Season with salt and pepper to taste, stir in the butter, and serve hot.

VELOUTÉ DE PATATE DOUCE AU GINGEMBRE

SWEET POTATO AND GINGER CREAM SOUP

There are many types of sweet potatoes, but until I moved to Europe, I'd never seen an orange-fleshed potato. I think this recipe is best made with the purple-skinned, white-fleshed sweet potatoes – but the orange-fleshed variety works well too. This recipe combines the sweetness of the potato with a kick to shake the cold off your body.

Serves 4

2 tbsp butter
1 lb (500 g) sweet potatoes, peeled and cut into chunks
1 leek, sliced
2 garlic cloves, crushed
1 quart (32 fl oz/1 liter) chicken stock
2-inch (5-cm) piece fresh ginger, peeled and grated
salt and freshly ground black pepper
4 tbsp (2 fl oz/60 ml) crème fraîche

Melt the butter in a pot over medium heat, add the sweet potatoes, leek, and garlic and cook for about 8 minutes. Add the stock and cook for 15 minutes. Add the ginger and salt and pepper and cook for 20 minutes more.

Blend until smooth, then return to the pot and cook over low heat for 5 minutes. Stir in the crème fraîche and serve hot.

BREADFRUIT CREAM SOUP

One of my favorite soups; I could make this in my sleep. It's the ultimate comfort soup—thick, rich, and creamy.

Serves 4

1 lb (500 g) breadfruit
7 tbsp (4 oz/100 g) butter
2 onions, finely chopped
5 garlic cloves, crushed
1¾-oz (50-g) slab smoked bacon,
   cubed
1 Scotch bonnet chile, finely chopped
2 sprigs parsley, finely chopped
2 cups (16 fl oz/500 ml) water
3 tbsp milk
4 cloves
salt and freshly ground black pepper
⅔ cup (5 fl oz/150 ml) crème fraîche

Peel the breadfruit, remove and discard the core, and cut the flesh into small cubes.

Melt the butter in a pot over medium heat, add the onions, garlic, bacon, chile, and parsley and cook until the onions have softened, about 5 minutes.

Add the breadfruit, water, milk, cloves, and salt and pepper. Cover the pot and simmer for 25 minutes.

Blend until smooth, then return the purée to the pot and cook over low heat for 10 minutes. Stir in the crème fraîche and serve hot.

CONGO SOUP

Most of the slaves that were brought to Guadeloupe and Martinique came from the Congo. Modern Creole still contains plenty of elements from the Bantu languages these slaves brought with them from Africa. This soup is a tribute to our history and is usually consumed during the rainy season.

Serves 6

14 oz (400 g) salted beef or
  corned beef
4 salted pigs' tails
1½ quarts (48 fl oz/1.5 liters) water
7 oz (200 g) frozen green pigeon peas
  (gungo peas), or drained canned
  pigeon peas
7 oz (200 g) frozen lima beans, or
  drained canned lima beans
7 oz (200 g) frozen hyacinth beans
  (green Indian beans), or fava beans
2 tbsp sunflower oil
1 large true yam (about 1.5kg/3lb 5oz),
  peeled and cut into chunks
8 oz (250 g) calabaza (West Indian
  pumpkin) or butternut squash,
  peeled and cut into chunks
2 small malangas (eddo) or dasheen
  (taro), peeled and cut into chunks
3 white-fleshed sweet potatoes,
  peeled and cut into chunks
1 onion, chopped
5 garlic cloves, chopped
1 bouquet garni
3 cloves
salt and freshly ground black pepper

Rinse the salted or corned beef and pigs' tails in cold water. Cut the meat into chunks and chop the pigs' tails into pieces through the joints. Put them in a pot, add the water, bring to a boil, and boil for 20 minutes. Drain the meat, reserving the broth.

Meanwhile, if using frozen pigeon peas and beans, put them in a bowl and cover with boiling water for a few minutes. Drain and rinse the beans.

Heat the oil in a pot and add the beans, all the vegetables, garlic, bouquet garni, cloves, and the meat and its broth. Bring to a boil and boil for about 10 minutes, then cover and simmer for 1½ hours, or until the pigeon peas have burst and are tender. Season with salt and pepper to taste and serve hot.

SOUPE GRASSE

FAT SOUP

In Guadeloupe and Martinique, this is *the* Sunday evening soup. After a heavy Sunday lunch, we don't need another big meal. It's called fat soup because we love to use really fatty meats to make it. You invariably will have fat soup on a Sunday: if you don't make it yourself, you'll go to someone's house and you're sure to come home with a bowl. It's a tradition. There are many ways of making this soup; this is my version.

Serves 4

3 tbsp vegetable oil
2 lb (1 kg) braising beef and bony
   cuts such as chuck, short rib, hock,
   oxtail, and cow's foot, chopped
   into large chunks
1 onion, sliced
1 bay leaf
2 sprigs parsley
2 sprigs thyme
3 garlic cloves, crushed
salt and freshly ground black pepper
1½ quarts (48 fl oz/1.5 liters) water
3 carrots, diced
2 parsnips, diced
5–7 oz (150–200 g) calabaza
   (West Indian pumpkin) or
   butternut squash, peeled and diced
2 leeks, diced
2 ribs celery, diced
¼ green cabbage, chopped
2 cloves
1 handful vermicelli pasta

Heat 2 tablespoons of the oil in a pot over medium-high heat and brown the meat thoroughly all over.

Add the onion, bay leaf, parsley, thyme, garlic, and salt and pepper and cover with the water. Bring to a boil over low heat, skimming off the foam that appears on the surface.

Add all the vegetables and the cloves and simmer over very low heat for 2–3 hours, skimming regularly to remove the foam.

Add the vermicelli, 1 tablespoon oil, and salt and pepper and simmer for 20 minutes. Serve hot.

COCONUT POTAGE

Everyone who knows me well knows I'm a sucker for coconuts. This is quite light and I can drink a whole pot of it on my own in a heartbeat. You really need to buy a coconut and make your own coconut milk (see p. 31) for this soup.

Serves 2

1 coconut, milked (p. 31)
2 cups (16 fl oz/500 ml) vegetable
   stock
¼ Scotch bonnet chile, very finely
   chopped
salt and freshly ground black pepper
1 pinch Colombo powder (p. 41)
1 pinch grated nutmeg
2 sprigs parsley, finely chopped
⅞ cup (7 fl oz/200 ml) crème fraîche

Pour the coconut milk, stock, and chile into a large pot. Add salt and pepper, the Colombo powder, and a pinch of nutmeg. Cook over medium heat for 20 minutes.

Mix the parsley with the crème fraîche and stir it into the soup before serving.

PIGEON PEAS SOUP

Ever heard of *Erwtensoep*? It's a traditional Dutch split pea soup and it's strikingly similar to this pigeon peas soup. Until I had *Erwtensoep* when I visited Holland, I never realized Creole food had any Dutch roots. I make this as a creamy soup, but the traditional Caribbean version that is so close to the Dutch one would skip the blending stage at the end.

Serves 4

10 oz (300 g) frozen green pigeon peas (gungo peas), or drained canned pigeon peas
1 quart (32 fl oz/1 liter) water
2 garlic cloves, crushed and finely chopped
2 tbsp sunflower oil
5½-oz (150-g) slab smoked bacon, rinsed and diced
1 lb (500 g) true yam, peeled and diced
8 oz (250 g) calabaza (West Indian pumpkin) or butternut squash, peeled and diced
2 onions, chopped
1 green onion, chopped
2 sprigs parsley, chopped
2 sprigs thyme
1 Scotch bonnet chile
salt and freshly ground black pepper
⅞ cup (7 fl oz/200 ml) canned coconut milk

If using frozen peas, put them in a bowl and cover with boiling water for a few minutes. Drain and rinse.

Put the peas in a pot with the water and garlic, cover, bring to a boil, and boil for about 30 minutes.

Heat the oil in a small frying pan and cook the bacon for about 3 minutes. Add the bacon to the peas. Add the yam, calabaza, onions, green onion, parsley, thyme, and the whole chile. Cover and cook over medium heat for 15 minutes.

Season with salt and pepper to taste and continue cooking until the soup thickens, about 15 minutes.

Remove the chile and thyme and blend until smooth. Add the coconut milk and return to the heat for 10 minutes. Serve hot.

SÔSS É KONDIMAN

SAUCES AND CONDIMENTS

◆◆◆◆◆◆◆◆◆◆

These sauces combine chiles and garlic with other flavors;
they are meant to take your food up a notch. You'll always
find at least one of them on a Creole table; if they are
missing, someone will be sure to ask for them.

SAUCE CHIEN

Many people have wondered why this is called "dog sauce." Some suggested it's because it's a bit of a random sauce that you can use for everything – marinade, dip, dressing – and follows you everywhere. Others thought the man who invented it was called Chien. I recently found out that the sauce gets its name from the knife used to chop the ingredients: the *coûteau Chien* (a brand name, meaning "dog knife") has been manufactured by the coûtellerie Pitelet in the city of Thiers, in central France, since 1880 and is still very popular in Guadeloupe, Martinique, French Guiana, and Réunion Island.

Makes about 1 lb (500 g)

1 onion, very finely chopped
2 green onions, very finely chopped
2 garlic cloves, very finely chopped
1 habanero chile, very finely chopped
1 tomato, very finely chopped
2 sprigs parsley, finely chopped
4 tbsp sunflower oil
juice of 1 lime
salt and freshly ground black pepper
¼ cup (2 fl oz/60 ml) hot water

Combine all the chopped ingredients, then pour in the oil and lime juice. Season with salt and pepper to taste, mix well, then add the hot water, stir, and serve right away or cover and keep in the refrigerator for 2 days.

SAUCE CRÉOLE

HOT CREOLE SAUCE

If you can really handle chile, this is what you pour over your grilled meat and fish.

Makes about 12 oz (375 g)

2 onions, roughly chopped
2 garlic cloves, peeled
1 habanero chile
3 tbsp sunflower oil
juice of 1 lime
salt and freshly ground black pepper

Put the onion, garlic, and the whole chile in a food processor and blend for about 20 seconds. Pour in the oil and lime juice and blend for 10 seconds. Season with salt and pepper to taste. Pour into a jar and serve right away or cover and keep in the refrigerator for 2 days.

CRÈME D'AVOCAT

AVOCADO CREAM

This spread is amazing in a Creole-style bruschetta with saltfish chiquetaille (p. 75) or smoked herring chiquetaille (p. 92). In a sandwich, as a dip, as a side, in your bokit (p. 100): the possibilities are endless.

Serves 4–6

2 large ripe green avocados
2 garlic cloves, crushed
1 sprig parsley, chopped
¼ habanero chile, chopped
juice of 1 lime
salt and freshly ground black pepper

Cut the avocados in half, pit, and scoop out the flesh. Place in a food processor and add the garlic, parsley, chile, and lime juice. Blend until smooth. Season with salt and pepper to taste. Serve right away.

PRESERVED CHILES

Back home there's always one person who can never have enough chile. The food is never spicy enough; it needs more kick. In my house this person is my mother. She told me a story that when she was studying in Bordeaux and ate at the canteen, she had a small jar of this stuff in a bag that she took out when it was time to eat. Hilarious!

Makes about two 14-oz (440-g) jars

20 habanero chiles
salt and freshly ground black pepper
2 onions, roughly chopped
4 garlic cloves, crushed
5 bay leaves
10 cloves
5 sprigs thyme
2 cups (16 fl oz/500 ml) vegetable oil
2 cups (16 fl oz/500 ml) white vinegar

Cut the chiles in half and put them into sterilized jars. Add salt and pepper, the onions, garlic, bay leaves, cloves, and thyme. Pour in the oil and vinegar, and add a little more salt and pepper.

Macerate for at least a week before using. Keep in the refrigerator for up to 6 months. Always use a clean spoon to avoid contamination.

PURÉE DE PIMENT

CHILE PURÉE

A very fiery sauce. Serve in a small dish for the brave and those who want to give their dishes a kick.

Makes about 12 oz (375 g)

12 habanero chiles
2 garlic cloves
1 onion, roughly chopped
1 Maggi or bouillon cube
juice of 1 lime
1 tbsp vegetable oil

Blend the chiles, garlic, onion, Maggi cube, and lime juice in a food processor until evenly mixed.

Heat the oil in a saucepan over low heat and pour in the chile purée. Cover and simmer for 3–4 minutes.

Leave to cool, then pour into a jar and place in the refrigerator for about 1 hour. Ideally, eat on the same day.

194   SAUCES AND CONDIMENTS

SYRUPS

◆◆◆◆◆◆◆◆◆◆

These will make your cocktails and desserts taste heavenly.
If you are feeling daring, try them drizzled over salads;
passion fruit and grenadine work especially well.

CANE SYRUP

Cane syrup is everywhere in Creole food. It's in cocktails, in desserts, and if you want to caramelize your meat, you can add a few tablespoons of cane syrup. You basically have to have a bottle of this in your kitchen. Crucial!

**Makes about 1 quart
(32 fl oz/1 liter)**

generous 4 cups (2 lb/1 kg) raw sugar
5 cups (40 fl oz/1.2 liters) water
juice of 2 limes
2 pinches grated cinnamon
1 pinch grated nutmeg
1 vanilla pod, cut in half lengthwise

Put the sugar in a large saucepan and add the water. Add the lime juice, cinnamon, nutmeg, and vanilla pod. Cook over low heat for about 25 minutes, stirring continuously with a wooden spoon, until the sugar has completely dissolved.

Remove the vanilla pod and leave to cool.

Using a funnel, pour the syrup into a sterilized bottle. Keep in the refrigerator for up to 3 months.

SIROP DE GROSEILLE

SORREL (HIBISCUS) SYRUP

This is the basis of the Christmas punch. You use it to make a *ti' punch* (p. 54), replacing the sugar or cane syrup with this bad boy. Festive flavors all the way!

**Makes about 1½ quarts
(48 fl oz/1.5 liters)**

1 lb (500 g) dried sorrel (hibiscus) petals, or 2 lb (1 kg) fresh sorrel when in season
zest of 1 lime, peeled in strips, plus the juice for soaking
2 quarts (64 fl oz/2 liters) water
2½ cups (19 oz/600 g) raw sugar
1 cinnamon stick
1 whole nutmeg, grated

If using fresh sorrel, soak the flowers in cold water with the juice of a lime for about 10 minutes. Drain the water. Peel the sorrel by discarding the core and keeping the petals.

Whether dried or fresh, place the petals in a large pot and cover with the water. Bring to a boil and boil for about 45 minutes. Strain, reserving the cooking water.

Put the sorrel water in a pot, add the sugar, cinnamon stick, nutmeg, and lime zest and simmer for 1 hour.

Leave to cool, then pour into a sterilized large airtight jar or empty rum bottles. Keep in the refrigerator for up to a month.

TIP

This makes a thick syrup. If you want it to be a bit more runny, add about 2 cups (16 fl oz/500 ml) more water when boiling the sorrel.

GRENADINE SYRUP

When I moved to England, it was difficult to find grenadine syrup. I decided to make my own. Crucial for your planteur cocktail (p. 62), it can also be drunk with ice and water or soda and lemonade, or poured over ice cream. A few online shops now sell grenadine syrup, brighter pink to look good in your cocktails but not as flavorsome. In fact some are just red sugar syrup, nothing to do with pomegranate fruit. This recipe is the real thing.

**Makes about 1¼ cups
(10 fl oz/300 ml)**

1½ cups (12 fl oz/350 ml) 100% pure pomegranate juice
¾ cup (6 oz/175 g) raw sugar
juice of ½ lime

Put the pomegranate juice in a saucepan and bring to a boil. Add the sugar and lime juice and stir until the sugar has dissolved. Simmer for 45 minutes.

Leave to cool, then pour into a sterilized jar or an empty rum bottle. Keep in the refrigerator for up to 3 months.

PASSION FRUIT SYRUP

My favorite juice is passion fruit. I love this syrup so much I often have it with cold water and ice with a lime wedge. When we were little, my brother and I would cut a passion fruit in half and share it. We'd pour in a tablespoon of cane syrup (p. 198) and eat it with a teaspoon as a snack. We picked our passion fruits from the climbing plant that grew all over one side of the house. It's the simple things that make the warmest memories.

**Makes about 1¼ cups
(10 fl oz/300 ml)**

20 fresh passion fruits, or 1 cup (8 fl oz/250 ml) passion fruit juice
1 vanilla pod, cut in half lengthwise
⅔ cup (5 oz/150 g) raw sugar
juice of 1 lime
⅔ cup (5 fl oz/150 ml) water

If using fresh passion fruits, cut them in half and scoop out the pulp into a saucepan or pour in the juice. Using a small knife, scrape the seeds from the vanilla pod and add to the pan, together with the sugar, lime juice, and water. Bring to a boil over medium-high heat, stirring until the sugar has dissolved. Simmer for 10 minutes, until it becomes syrupy.

Leave to cool, then pour into a sterilized jar or an empty rum bottle. Keep in the refrigerator for up to a month.

DÉSSÈ

DESSERTS

◆◆◆◆◆◆◆◆◆◆◆◆

Creole food has so much to choose from when it comes
to sweet things. There's a huge array of tropical fruits,
and these are often combined with French techniques
to make desserts you'd never dream of. Sometimes the
simplest things make the perfect finale for an exotic dinner;
sometimes an impressive cake is needed for a celebration.
These are a few of my favorite desserts.

BANANA AND RUM FRITTERS

Carnival equals sweet fritters. These treats are served every Sunday throughout January and until Ash Wednesday.

Makes 20–30 fritters

4 ripe bananas
¼ cup (2 oz/60 g) raw sugar
2 eggs
1 cup (4 oz/125 g) all-purpose flour
1 tsp baking powder
1 vanilla pod, cut in half lengthwise
grated zest of 1 lime
1 pinch grated cinnamon
1 pinch grated nutmeg
1 tbsp white rum
1 quart (32 fl oz/1 liter) sunflower oil
1 tbsp confectioners' sugar

Peel the bananas, put them in a bowl, and mash with a fork. Whisk in the sugar and eggs, then the flour and baking powder. Using a small knife, scrape the seeds from the vanilla pod and add to the mixture, then stir in the lime zest, cinnamon, nutmeg, and rum.

In a deep pan, heat the oil over medium heat until it reaches 350°F (180°C), or until a cube of bread browns in 30–40 seconds. Make sure the oil doesn't get too hot and start to smoke. Gently drop tablespoonfuls of the batter into the oil and cook for about 2 minutes on each side, turning occasionally, until dark golden all over.

Scoop the fritters out of the oil and drain on paper towels. Sprinkle with confectioners' sugar and serve hot.

TIP

I like to add a tablespoon
of unsweetened dried coconut
to my banana fritters
to add texture.

DESSERTS

TOURMENT D'AMOUR

LOVE TORMENT

This recipe is from Les Saintes, two small islands that form part of the archipelago of Guadeloupe. Most of the men on the islands were fishermen, and their wives would make these cakes to show how tormented they were while their husbands were away at sea and how happy they were to have them back. The recipe requires organization and careful preparation. But you'll see why the fishermen were looking forward to their wives' cakes.

Makes 6–8 cakes

Coconut jam
2 coconuts, finely grated
    (approximately 10 oz/300 g)
2½ cups (19 oz/600 g) raw sugar
2 cups (16 fl oz/500 ml) water
1 cinnamon stick
1 pinch grated nutmeg
grated zest of 1 lime
1 vanilla pod, cut in half lengthwise

butter, for greasing
19 oz (600 g) prepared pie dough

Crème pâtissière
1 cup (8 fl oz/250 ml) milk
3 tbsp (2 oz/50 g) superfine sugar
1 egg
2 tbsp cornstarch
2 tbsp rum
1 tsp grated cinnamon
½ tsp grated nutmeg
grated zest of 1 lime
½ vanilla pod

Sponge
4 eggs
⅞ cup (7 oz/200 g) superfine sugar
1⅔ cups (7 oz/200 g) all-purpose flour
⅞ cup (7 oz/200 g) unsalted butter,
    melted
½ vanilla pod
1 pinch grated cinnamon
1 pinch grated nutmeg
1 tbsp rum

Make the coconut jam first. Put the grated coconut in a saucepan with the sugar, water, cinnamon stick, nutmeg, and lime zest. Using a small knife, scrape the seeds from the vanilla pod into the mixture and add the pod. Cover and cook over medium-high heat, stirring until the sugar has dissolved and skimming regularly to remove the foam. Cook until the jam has thickened, about 10 minutes. Leave to cool, then spoon into a sterilized jar.

Grease 6–8 deep fluted tartlet pans, about 4 inches (10 cm) in diameter. Roll out the dough and line the pans. Prick the dough all over with a fork. Spread a layer of coconut jam over the pastry, then put the pastry shells in the refrigerator.

To make the crème pâtissière, bring the milk to a boil in a saucepan. In a mixing bowl, whisk the sugar and egg together until the mixture thickens slightly, then add the cornstarch and whisk until evenly mixed. Whisk in the hot milk, then return the mixture to the pan and cook over low heat, whisking continuously until it's thick and starts bubbling up. Remove from the heat and add the rum, cinnamon, nutmeg, and lime zest; scrape the seeds from the vanilla pod into the mixture. Leave to cool.

Preheat the oven to 350°F (180°C).

To make the sponge, beat the eggs with the sugar until light and fluffy. Whisk in the flour. Whisking continuously, add the melted butter. Add the seeds scraped from the vanilla pod, the cinnamon, nutmeg, and rum.

Take your tartlet pans out of the refrigerator and divide the crème pâtissière among them, spreading it in a thin layer that covers the jam completely. Add the sponge batter, but do not overfill, as the cake will swell up as it bakes. Bake until well risen and golden, 60 minutes.

Leave to cool before removing from the pans.

MONT BLANC COCONUT CAKE

This is my favorite cake. I have tasted many versions but none ever came close to the one my mum makes. I learned this recipe when I begged her to make it on Sunday afternoons. I can honestly say that this is where I get my passion for coconuts. I have simplified her recipe, but you do need to make a génoise sponge cake. The génoise gives a light and airy feel that makes it taste like a coconut cloud.

Serves 6

butter, for greasing

Génoise sponge
4 eggs, separated
1 pinch salt
1 cup (4 oz/125 g) all-purpose flour
1 tsp baking powder
2 pinches grated cinnamon
1 pinch grated nutmeg
generous ½ cup (4 oz/125 g)
    superfine sugar

Coconut cream
1⅔ cups (13 fl oz/400 ml) coconut
    milk
1 can (about 14 oz/400 g) condensed
    milk
2 tbsp cornstarch
6 tbsp (3 fl oz/100 ml) water
1 tbsp rum
grated zest of 1 lime

1 tbsp rum

To decorate
1 coconut
glacé cherries (optional)

Preheat the oven to 350°F (180°C). Grease and line a 9½-inch (24 cm) round cake pan with parchment paper.

First make the sponge cake. In a mixing bowl, beat the egg whites with the salt until stiff peaks form. Sift the flour, baking powder, and spices into another mixing bowl. When the egg whites are stiff, add the sugar and carry on whisking. Once the mixture is firm, add the egg yolks, whisking continuously. Still whisking, add the sifted flour mixture and carry on whisking for another 2–3 minutes. Pour the batter into the prepared pan and place in the oven until well risen, with a nice golden top, 20–25 minutes.

Remove the cake from the oven and leave to cool in its pan.

To make the coconut cream, pour the coconut milk, condensed milk, cornstarch, and water into a saucepan and simmer for a few minutes, stirring constantly, until thick and creamy. Add the rum and lime zest and leave to cool.

When the cake is cool, turn it out onto a piece of wax paper. Slice it in half horizontally and place the cut sides facing up. Sprinkle 1 tbsp rum over the cut sides. Spread some of the coconut cream evenly over both sides, then sandwich them together. Spread the remaining coconut cream over the top of the cake and all around the sides.

To decorate, break open the coconut and scoop out the meat. Peel and discard the brown skin. Wash the coconut meat under cold water and then grate it finely. Sprinkle the coconut all over the cake until it is completely covered. Scatter glacé cherries on top, if desired. Place it in the refrigerator for at least 4 hours before serving.

FLAMBÉ BANANAS

The most popular dessert in Guadeloupe and Martinique. It's traditionally made with ordinary bananas, but we found them too soft and so my mum made a firmer version, using ripe plantains. It became a family recipe. When my sister and I lived in Paris, I would make these when I missed home – and my sister couldn't get enough. When she makes them, she uses cane syrup (p. 198) instead of sugar and adds vanilla.

Serves 4

2 very ripe plantains
3 tbsp butter
1 pinch grated cinnamon
1 pinch grated nutmeg
⅔ cup (5 oz/150 g) raw sugar
juice of 1 lime
3–4 tbsp white rum

Peel the plantains and slice them in thirds lengthwise. Melt the butter in a frying pan and fry the plantains on both sides, until golden.

Add the cinnamon, nutmeg, sugar, and lime juice. Pour the rum into the pan and immediately – standing well back as the flames leap up – either tilt the pan slightly so it touches the flame (if you have a gas range) or hold a match near to the pan (on an electric range) to flambé the bananas. Serve immediately.

TIP

Grate a little lime zest over the bananas before serving, and serve with coconut or vanilla ice cream.

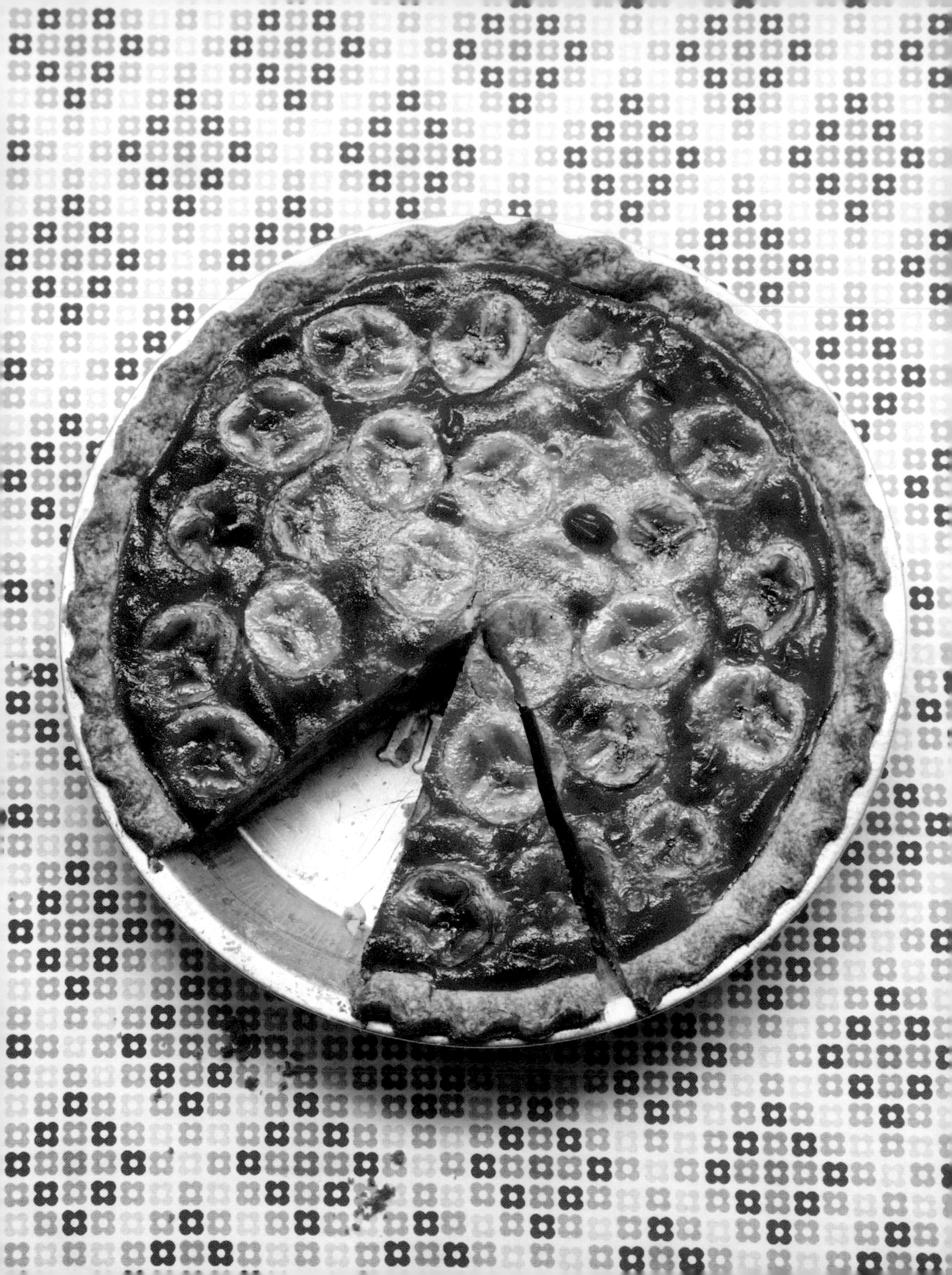

TARTE À LA BANANE

BANANA PIE

I re-explored this recipe at my supper club. There was something I didn't like about the way traditional banana pies were made back home: I realized it was because the bananas are often sliced too thinly, which makes them too soft and mushy. I like the texture of banana and wanted to feel it in the pie. This is my take on the traditional Creole banana pie.

Serves 6

butter, for greasing
flour, for dusting
about 10 oz (300 g) prepared
    pie dough
5 bananas
4 eggs
6 tbsp golden superfine sugar
1 vanilla pod, cut in half lengthwise
1¼ cups (10 fl oz/300 ml) heavy cream
1 pinch grated cinnamon
1 pinch grated nutmeg
1 tbsp rum

Preheat the oven to 400°F (200°C). Grease a 8½-inch (22-cm) tart pan.

On a lightly floured work surface, roll out the dough quite thin and line the tart pan. Prick the dough all over with a fork.

Peel the bananas and cut into rings about ⅜ inch (1 cm) thick, then arrange in a circle, one or two layers deep, on the pastry.

In a mixing bowl, whisk together the eggs and sugar until the sugar has dissolved. Using a small knife, scrape the seeds from the vanilla pod and add to the mixture, together with the cream, cinnamon, nutmeg, and rum. Pour the mixture over the bananas, then place the pie in the oven. When the pie starts to become golden, after about 30 minutes, reduce the heat to 350°F (180°C) and continue to bake for another 30 minutes, until the filling is firm to the touch. Leave to cool slightly before serving.

PEANUT CAKE

I have a love affair with this cake. My mother is from Marie-Galante, a small island that is part of the archipelago of Guadeloupe. There are things that you can get on Marie-Galante that you can't get anywhere else. *Gâteau pistache* is one of them.
We used to order this cake for celebrations, birthdays, and big parties, and we had to go and collect it from the boat. When I heard that the lady who made them had died, I was devastated. I probably made this cake a hundred times before successfully replicating the taste, but it was worth it. Not the easiest recipe but definitely a winner!

Serves 6

butter, for greasing

Génoise sponge
4 eggs, separated
1 pinch salt
1 cup (4 oz/125 g) all-purpose flour
1 tsp baking powder
generous ½ cup (4 oz/125 g) golden
    superfine sugar
3 pinches grated cinnamon
2 pinches grated nutmeg

7 oz (200 g) roasted peanuts, shelled
1 tsp vanilla extract

Peanut buttercream
5 tbsp (2½ fl oz/75 ml) water
½ cup (4 oz/100 g) golden superfine
    sugar
2 tsp vanilla sugar (p. 28)
2 eggs
1 cup (8 oz/250 g) butter, at room
    temperature, cut into cubes

Preheat the oven to 350°F (180°C). Grease and line a 9½-inch (24 cm) round cake pan.

First make the sponge cake. In a mixing bowl, beat the egg whites with the salt until stiff peaks form. Sift the flour and baking powder into another mixing bowl. When the egg whites are stiff, add the sugar and carry on whisking. Once the mixture is firm, add the egg yolks, whisking continuously. Still whisking, add the flour mixture, 2 pinches cinnamon, and 1 pinch nutmeg and carry on whisking for another 2–3 minutes. Pour the batter into the prepared pan and place in the oven until well risen, with a nice golden top, 20–25 minutes.

Remove the cake from the oven and leave to cool in its pan.

Put the peanuts on a baking sheet and roast them in the oven for 15 minutes, shaking the baking sheet regularly so they roast evenly. Leave to cool.

When the cake is cool, turn it out onto a piece of wax paper. Slice it in half horizontally and place it with the cut sides facing up. In a small bowl, mix the vanilla extract with the remaining pinch of cinnamon and nutmeg and sprinkle over the cut sides of the cake.

To make the peanut buttercream, heat the water, sugar, and vanilla sugar in a saucepan until the sugar has dissolved, then bring to a boil and boil until the syrup reaches 250°F (120°C); see Tip, p. 218. Meanwhile, put the eggs in a mixing bowl and whisk lightly. Gradually pour the hot syrup into the eggs, whisking continuously until the mixture has cooled down and is thick and smooth. Beat in the cubes of butter one by one until you have a smooth buttercream.

(continued)

Place ½ cup (2½ oz/70 g) of the peanuts in a food processor and blend to a powder. Add the powder to the buttercream. Spread some of the buttercream evenly over the bottom cake layer, then sandwich together with the top layer. Spread the remaining buttercream over the top of the cake and all around the sides. Place in the refrigerator for 30 minutes.

Put the remaining peanuts in the food processor and blitz briefly until the nuts are in chunky pieces. Remove the cake from the refrigerator and sprinkle the peanuts over the top and around the sides of the cake. Keep the cake in the refrigerator until ready to serve.

TIP

If you don't have a sugar thermometer, use the soft ball test to check when the syrup is at the right temperature: dip a teaspoon into the syrup and drop it into a glass of cold water. The syrup should form a small soft ball.

GATEAU PATATE

SWEET POTATO CAKE

This is a cake you can make when you crave something sweet and realize you don't have any flour. It's one of my favorite no-nonsense recipes. Enjoy it with a scoop of ice cream.

Serves 6

⅞ cup (7 oz/200 g) unsalted butter, melted, plus extra for greasing
2 lb (1 kg) sweet potatoes
3 eggs
3 tbsp rum
3 tbsp raw sugar
1 pinch grated cinnamon
1 pinch grated nutmeg

Preheat the oven to 375°F (190°C). Grease a 9½-inch (24-cm) round cake pan.

Peel the sweet potatoes and boil for 25 minutes. Squeeze out the water from the potatoes, then purée in a food processor. Add the melted butter, eggs, rum, sugar, cinnamon, and nutmeg. Mix thoroughly, then pour into the baking dish and bake for 1 hour. Leave to cool before serving.

COCONUT RICE PUDDING

My sister loves this recipe. She has the ability to create naughty recipes for late-night cravings. She's a night owl. She used to wake me up after bedtime, and we'd sneak into the kitchen for rice pudding or cornmeal porridge. This recipe is for those of you like my sister, whose belly wakes you up in the middle of the night.

Serves 4

1⅔ cups (13 fl oz/400 ml) coconut milk
1 vanilla pod, cut in half lengthwise
1 cinnamon stick
zest of 1 lime, peeled in strips
¾ cup (5 oz/150 g) Arborio rice
⅞ cup (7 oz/200 g) condensed milk

Put the coconut milk in a saucepan with the vanilla pod, cinnamon stick, and lime zest and bring to a boil. Once the milk starts boiling, add the rice. Stir, cover, and cook over low heat until all the coconut milk has been absorbed, about 30 minutes.

Pour in the condensed milk, stir, and leave over the heat for a minute, then pour the rice into a large bowl. Remove the vanilla pod, cinnamon, and lime zest and leave to cool.

Divide the rice among four ramekins and leave in the refrigerator for at least 1 hour before serving.

PINEAPPLE UPSIDE-DOWN CAKE

What's more Caribbean than a pineapple upside-down cake? Many of my students tell me they have found it difficult to make the sponge in the past: it comes out too hard, undercooked, or too flat. This recipe turns upside-down cake around and will make it your go-to recipe for a decadent treat.

Serves 6

1 cup plus 2 tbsp (8 oz/250 g) golden superfine sugar
1 ripe, very sweet pineapple, peeled, cored, and cut into slices about ⅜ inch (1 cm) thick, or 1 can (14 oz/400 g) pineapple rings, drained
4 eggs
1⅔ cups (7 oz/200 g) all-purpose flour
1 tsp baking powder
⅞ cup (7 oz/200 g) unsalted butter, very soft, but not liquid
2 tbsp rum
1 pinch grated cinnamon
1 pinch grated nutmeg
1 tsp vanilla extract

Preheat the oven to 400°F (200°C).

Put 4 tablespoons (2 oz/50 g) sugar and 1 tablespoon water in a 9½-inch (24 cm) round cake pan and place in the oven until the sugar caramelizes. Arrange the pineapple slices in the caramel.

In a large mixing bowl, whisk the eggs until they are light and fluffy. Whisk in the remaining sugar. Add the flour, baking powder, and butter and whisk until the batter is smooth. Add the rum, cinnamon, nutmeg, and vanilla.

Pour the batter over the pineapple slices and place in the oven. Bake until a skewer inserted into the center of the cake comes out clean, 40 minutes.

Remove from the oven and leave to cool in the pan.

To serve, place a large plate over the top of the cake pan, flip them upside down together, and lift off the cake pan.

COCONUT FLAN

Coconut flan is a traditional recipe in the Creole islands. My mother used to make it as a Sunday afternoon treat. She said the secret was in the timing and the bain-marie. If we were good, my sister, brother, and I would get two ramekins each. Very sweet and delicious.

Makes 6 flan

1 can (about 14 fl oz/400 g) condensed milk
1 can (about 12 fl oz/360 ml) evaporated milk
4 eggs, separated
1 pinch grated cinnamon
1 pinch grated nutmeg
finely grated zest of ½ lime, plus 1 tsp juice
1⅔ cups (13 fl oz/400 ml) canned coconut milk
1 tbsp unsweetened dried coconut (optional)
1/4 cup (2 oz/60 g) raw sugar
6 tbsp (3 fl oz/100 ml) water

Preheat the oven to 350°F (180°C).

In a bowl, combine the condensed milk, evaporated milk, and egg yolks and whisk together. Add the cinnamon, nutmeg, and lime zest. Gradually whisk in the coconut milk. Add the dried coconut, if using.

In another bowl, beat the egg whites until stiff peaks form. Gently fold in the coconut mixture.

Heat the sugar, lime juice, and water in a small heavy-bottomed saucepan over medium heat until it forms a deep brown caramel. Pour a little into six ramekins.

Put the ramekins in a deep ovenproof dish and pour in enough boiling water to reach halfway up the ramekins. Pour the coconut flan mixture into the ramekins and bake in the bain-marie for 35 minutes, until just set.

Leave to cool at room temperature, then put in the refrigerator for at least 2 hours before serving.

WINE PINEAPPLE

This recipe was an afternoon treat when we were children. It's well known to all children who grew up in the French Caribbean. Yes, the recipe contains wine – but the excuse would be that, compared to rum, wine is not strong, so children can have it. Not a very good excuse, but I wasn't complaining.

Serves 4

1 pineapple
¼ cup (2 oz/50 g) raw sugar
2 cups (16 fl oz/500 ml) red wine
2 pinches grated cinnamon
2 pinches grated nutmeg
1 tsp vanilla extract

Peel the pineapple. Cut it into quarters and remove the core. Cut the pineapple into chunks and place the pieces in a large bowl. Sprinkle the sugar over, then add the wine, spices, and vanilla. Stir, then place in the refrigerator for at least 2 hours before serving.

PÂTE DE GOYAVE

GUAVA CHEESE (GUAVA PASTE)

One of the things I used to pack in my suitcase when I flew away from home back to Europe was guava cheese. It's always in my cupboard. It can simply be spread on toast, but it's very versatile (see Tip), and now that I make my own, I often use it in baking.

Makes about 7 oz (200 g)

2 lb (1 kg) ripe pink-fleshed guavas
about 2 cups (1 lb/500 g) raw sugar
juice of ½ lime

Wash and quarter the guavas. Put them in a saucepan and add water to cover. Put the lid on and cook over medium heat, stirring regularly, until they are soft and easily pierced.

Scoop out the guava flesh with a slotted spoon and blend in a food processor until you have a smooth purée.

Weigh the purée (you should have around 1 lb/500 g) and weigh out an equal amount of sugar. Put the purée and sugar into a clean saucepan. Add the lime juice. Simmer until the mixture is thick enough to stay separated when stirred with a wooden spoon, 25–30 minutes. Pour onto a greased baking sheet for thin guava cheese or into a cake pan if you prefer thicker cubes of paste.

Leave to cool completely, then cut into cubes.

TIP

It's very sweet, but you can eat it on its own, just like I did as a child. You can also use it to glaze meat, bake with it (p. 226), or serve it with (dairy) cheese.

PÂTÉ GOYAVE

GUAVA PASTRY

When you go to the beach and swim and frolic in the sand, it makes you hungry. Very hungry. Fortunately, there are always a few market ladies around to cater to your hunger in the Caribbean. Their stalls offer refreshing icy "snowballs" and coconut sorbets, but also a large display of cakes, tarts, pies, and pastries. This guava pastry is a classic: if you see one of these stalls and they don't have it, they must have run out—no other reason!

Makes 8 pastries

2 cups (8 oz/250 g) all-purpose flour
½ cup (4 oz/125 g) unsalted butter,
  at room temperature
2 tbsp (1 oz/30 g) superfine sugar
1 tsp salt
⅞ cup (7 fl oz/200 ml) water
5 oz (150 g) guava cheese (p. 225)
  or quince paste
1 egg yolk, lightly beaten

Put the flour in a large mixing bowl and make a well in the center. Add the butter, sugar, salt, and water to the well. Mix and knead until you have a smooth ball of dough. Set aside for at least 2 hours.

Preheat the oven to 350°F (180°C).

Roll out the dough until it's ¹⁄₁₆ inch (2 mm) thick. Cut out 16 rectangles, 4 x 2 inches (10 x 5 cm). Place a 1½- to 2-inch (4–5 cm) piece of guava cheese in the center of 8 of the pieces of dough and cover them with the remaining pieces. Crimp the edges together with a fork and make three small cuts in the center of each. Brush with egg yolk. Bake until deep golden brown, 20 minutes. Leave to cool before serving.

TIP

Instead of guava cheese, you
can use banana jam (p. 228)
or coconut jam (p. 208).

BANANA PASTRY

I never knew why this pastry is called *jalousie* in Martinique; in Guadeloupe we just call it *tarte banane*. I've discovered that the classic French *jalousie* pastry is so called because the cuts in the top make it look like slatted blind called a *jalousie* (rather like a Venetian blind); I guess a jealous lover could spy through this type of blind. Whatever the story, I love eating it. You don't have to make rectangles; you can use round cutters instead – that's how this is made in Guadeloupe. You can also use guava cheese (p. 225) or coconut jam (p. 208) for a change.

Makes 4 pastries

Banana jam
1¼ cups (10 fl oz/300 ml) water
1⅓ cups (10 oz/300 g) raw sugar
juice of 1 lime
1 vanilla pod, cut in half lengthwise
2 ripe bananas
juice of 1 orange
1 tbsp rum

flour, for dusting
10 oz (300 g) puff pastry dough
1 egg yolk, lightly beaten

To make the banana jam, put the water, sugar, lime juice, and vanilla pod in a saucepan over low heat until you have a light brown syrup, about 8 minutes.

Peel the bananas and cut into rings about ¾ inch (2 cm) thick. Add the bananas and orange juice to the syrup and simmer for 20 minutes, stirring regularly to avoid it burning or sticking too much. Add the rum. Leave to cool.

Preheat the oven to 350°F (180°C).

On a lightly floured work surface, roll out the puff pastry to about ⅛ inch (4 mm) thick.

Cut out eight 4-inch (10-cm) squares. Place 1 tablespoon of banana jam in the center of 4 of the squares; be careful not to put too much. Cover each with another square and make two parallel cuts, about 2 inches (5 cm) long, in the top. Crimp the edges together with your fingers and brush with egg yolk. Bake until golden brown, 30 minutes. Leave to cool before serving.

MANGO GRATIN

This is easy! Very easy. I had my three-, four-, and seven-year-old nieces and nephew make this a few months ago. They were so happy when they realized they could cook. If you have nice colorful ramekins, this dessert will wow any guests. Why not chop some mint and sprinkle it over to finish?

Serves 4

2 mangoes
3 tbsp butter, plus extra for topping
5 tbsp (2½ fl oz/75 ml) aged rum
1 vanilla pod, cut in half lengthwise
1½ cups (12 fl oz/400 ml) coconut
 milk
3 tbsp raw sugar
grated zest of 1 lime

Preheat the oven to 425°F (220°C).

Peel and pit the mangoes and slice the flesh lengthwise. Melt the butter in a frying pan, add the mangoes, rum, and the seeds scraped from the vanilla pod, and cook until the mango begins to soften, 5–6 minutes.

Divide the pieces of mango among four ramekins and dot with butter. Pour 6 tablespoons (3 fl oz/100 ml) coconut milk into each ramekin and sprinkle each with one-fourth of the sugar and the lime zest.

Place in the hot oven for about 3 minutes. Leave to cool before serving.

GLOSSARY

◆◆◆◆◆◆◆◆◆◆◆◆◆◆◆◆◆◆◆◆◆◆◆◆◆◆◆

Accras (also spelled *acras*, *akras*)

Small fritters, generally made with either fish or vegetables, the most widespread form being saltfish. Originally from West Africa and made with black-eyed peas or vegetables.

Achiote (known locally as *roucou*)

Red dried seeds from a tree native to the Caribbean and South America. Achiote is the most authentic spice on the islands, as it was used by the Amerindians before the arrival of the Europeans. The Amerindians also used it to paint their bodies, and it's now mainly used to color cooking oil to make Creole fish court bouillon (p. 110), and to make red butter *(beurre rouge* or *bè rouj)*, a red-orange, salty, spicy lard made with ground achiote seeds, which is sold in jars and loose at market stalls.

Aji dulce (also known as sweet habanero pepper)

The Spanish name means "sweet chile." A member of the *Capsicum chinense* family, aji dulce has an aroma and flavor complex similar to that of the red habanero, but without the intense heat.

Bacon (known locally as *lard fumé*)

We use smoked bacon for flavor in many recipes, especially stews. It can be smoked fatback, smoked pork belly, thick-cut smoked bacon, or thick lardons cut from a smoked bacon slab.

Bakes

A type of fried dough bread from Trinidad.

Baton kako (also known as *bwa kako* in Martinique)

A stick of pure cocoa paste. Used to make hot chocolate and a crucial element of the *pain au beurre et chocolat* served at celebrations in Martinique. The best Martiniquais chocolate is made out of this pure cocoa that retains all the natural flavors, aromas, and qualities of pure cocoa mass and cocoa butter.

Baton lélé (also known as *bois lélé, bwa lélé*)

A small stick with three or five branches at the end used to whisk or stir drinks and food. Often made from the wood of cocoa trees. Small *batons lélés* are used to stir ti' punch and coconut punch: bigger ones are used a bit like a potato masher, to stir *giraumonade, calalou* or *migan*.

Beans and peas

"Beans" and "peas" mean the same thing in the Caribbean. Rice and peas is rice and beans. Widely used in Creole cuisine, each variety has a specific taste and – if you want to make an authentic dish – one cannot be substituted for another. They are usually available in both dried and canned forms.

Blaff

Fish, shellfish, or meat poached in an aromatic broth of herbs and spices. Blaff is supposedly the sound the fish or meat makes when you drop it into the broth. See pp. 104, 115 and 141.

Bokit

A ball of fried dough filled with anything from meat (p. 100) to fish, most commonly chicken and saltfish. Bokit'la, a London-based street food company, sells them in markets across the city. You can also find bokits in many French cities.

Boucan

From the Amerindian language, meaning "wood grill," a type of fire on which Caribs smoked meat and fish. It also designates the hut in which they did the smoking. Rather than quick grilling, it implies slow cooking over charcoal.

Breadfruit

Round, with a rough green skin and a cream to yellow flesh, breadfruit is a member of the mulberry family. It's the potatoes of the Caribbean. Very starchy, it can be boiled, fried, puréed, roasted. You can find it in exotic markets in large cities from June to October; it is also available in cans.

Calabash

A round gourd, mainly used as a utensil after its flesh has been removed. The usage was inherited from the Amerindians and in the kitchen it is used as cups, bowls, spoons, to store spices, carry water, marinate fish – pretty much anything that needs a container.

Calabaza (also known as Caribbean or West Indian pumpkin, locally known as *giraumon*)

A Caribbean variety of a very large pumpkin with bright orange flesh and very large seeds. Sold in slices at exotic markets. It's used in stews and soups and in a Creole recipe called *giraumonade* (p. 171). Its cousin, butternut squash, can be substituted.

Calalou (also spelled *calallou, callaloo*)

A soup made of callaloo leaves (dasheen or taro leaves), also known as kale, Chinese spinach, or ong choy (which can easily be replaced by fresh spinach leaves). It's a classic Caribbean soup that varies from one island to another. The soup often contains okra and pork meats like snout, bacon slab, and pigs' tails; in the French islands, crab is used.

Cassava (also known as manioc, yucca)

A tuber with dark brown rough skin that looks like a log. There are sweet and sour varieties of cassava; both are poisonous when raw. Cassava use is inherited from the Amerindians and is used to make flour (for flatbreads and crepes), and tapioca and is also boiled and eaten as a vegetable.

Chatrou

Octopus in Guadeloupe and Martinique.

Chaudeau

A speciality from Guadeloupe, *chaudeau* is a mix of eggs, milk, and spices, between a drink and a dessert. It is served at weddings, christenings, and first communions, and its preparation is steeped in ritual: for instance, nothing else can be prepared in the same kitchen at the same time, and the person preparing it cannot be on her time of the month. A good *chaudeau* is a sign of a successful party.

Chiquetaille

Shredded salted fish or meat marinated with herbs, onions, garlic, lime, and chile. See p. 75 and 92.

Chocho (also known as chayote, chow chow, mirliton, christophine)

An edible plant, a gourd, and a cousin of cucumber, originally from South America. It's pear-shaped, and its color can range from cream to light green. Its flesh can be eaten raw, but its core must be cooked. It tends to be consumed boiled and, in the French Caribbean, in gratins. The flesh is soft and watery. You can replace chocho with zucchini or cucumbers.

Colombo

A spice mix unique to the French Caribbean that gave its name to a curry dish made with chicken, pork, mutton, lamb, or even root vegetables. It is usually in powder form but can also be found as a paste in the French Caribbean. You can make your own (p. 41) or replace it with regular curry powder if you don't have access to all the spices.

Conch (known locally as *lambi*)

A mollusk that lives in a spiral-shaped seashell. Its very firm white flesh needs to be pounded to soften it before it is grilled as the Amerindians did or stewed in red sauce. Its shell is used as a horn in carnival celebrations. Conch is now a protected species, and it can be difficult to find.

Court bouillon

A cooking technique, primarily used to prepare red tropical fish. Creole court bouillon is a tomato-based broth in which the fish is poached. Not to be confused with the traditional French court bouillon. See p. 110.

Dasheen (also known as taro, locally known as *madère* in Guadeloupe, *dachine* in Martinique)

A tuber with dark brown skin. This root has a white, sometimes purplish flesh and is part of what is called ground provision or hard food. It's usually boiled, and both the root and its leaves can be eaten (*see* Calalou).

Dutch oven

The type of pot you need to cook Creole stews. Usually made of cast iron or aluminium, it has a well-fitting lid and distributes heat to the food very slowly and evenly. You can easily find one online or at Afro-Caribbean markets.

Féroce

A dish made from avocado, salted cod, cassava flour, and quite a lot of hot chile pepper, which makes it ferocious indeed. See pp. 66 and 68.

Giraumon: *see* Calabaza

Ground provisions (also known as hard food)

The term covers vegetables such as yams, breadfruit, green bananas, plantains, cassava, dasheen (taro), and sweet potatoes. They are usually boiled and served as side dishes.

Guava

Pear-shaped fruit with a pink or white flesh that ripens from green to yellow. They are sweet and often used to make juice, punch, jam, jelly, and paste for baking. See p. 225.

Malanga (eddo)

A tuber with dark brown skin; very similar to dasheen (taro) but smaller.

Matété (Guadeloupe) or Matoutou (Martinique)

A traditional rice dish made with blue land crab; usually eaten on Easter Monday. See p. 120.

Migan

A very-easy-to-make dish, typical of the French islands. Its traditional base is breadfruit and pumpkin with pork meats. See p. 133.

Okra (also known as ladies' fingers, locally known as *gombo*)

An edible green pod with white seeds. The base of many African and Caribbean stews, it can be quite slimy when cooked. It's high in fiber, vitamin C, and antioxidants. Widely available from supermarkets.

Ouassou (Guadeloupe), z'habitant (Martinique)

A variety of prawn local to the Caribbean islands. It lives in freshwater close to the source of rivers. Its name in Guadeloupe is derived from the French *roi des sources* (king of sources), which became *ouassou*. In Martinique it's called *z'habitant*, meaning "inhabitant of sources." It can be compared to crayfish in that it lives in freshwater and has large claws. It is also called giant river prawn, giant freshwater prawn, Malaysian prawn, freshwater scampi, or Rosenberg prawn.

They are really hard to find outside the Caribbean and were replaced in the recipes by jumbo shrimp or other types of shrimp.

Pain au beurre et chocolat

A Martinique classic. One doesn't work without the other. It literally means "butter bread and chocolate." The *pain au beurre* is a local braided brioche that takes hours and a flair to make. It is served with hot chocolate made with pure cocoa and is the thing that will dictate whether your christening, first communion, or wedding celebration is a success.

Pâté en pot

A Martinique institution: a very thick soup made with offal, vegetables, and capers, it's made for all types of celebrations. See p. 176.

Plantain

It's a banana, but not a fruit—a vegetable always cooked before eating. It starts off green and hard and ripens to yellow, then black.

Rhum agricole

This literally means "agricultural rum," as opposed to industrially produced rum. Rhum agricole is distilled from freshly squeezed sugarcane juice rather than molasses. It is produced in Guadeloupe, Martinique, and Haiti.

Saltfish

Fish that is salt-cured and dried. In the Caribbean, it is almost universally understood to mean salted cod. It could be any fish, although it does tend to be whitefish such as cod or pollock. But herring, shark, and snapper, among others, can also be saltfish.

Shrubb

A liqueur made from rum infused with orange peel and sugar, traditionally drunk at Christmas. Why is it spelled with two *b*'s? Not sure why, but that's Creole! See p. 52.

Sorrel (also known as roselle or hibiscus, locally known as *groseille pays*)

The flower of the *Hibiscus sabdariffa* is used to make syrup, jelly, and punch, especially during the Christmas season in the Caribbean. It comes from West Africa, where it's called *bissap*, and it is widely used around the world as the base for herbal teas, especially those with a pinky-red color and flavored with berries.

Dried sorrel is available all year-round in Afro-Caribbean shops, and fresh sorrel can be found in the month or two leading up to Christmas in these same shops. It is also sold as hibiscus flowers in Latin, Turkish, and Persian shops.

Souskay (also know as *souskaï*)

A dish named after the preparation technique, which entails soaking fruits in a savory vinaigrette of lime, garlic, salt, and chile. See p. 84.

Yam

The true yam (not to be confused with the orange-fleshed sweet potato) is a very large tuber with thick, rough, dark brown skin. The starchy flesh can be either white or yellow, the yellow-fleshed variety being the most widely available in the Caribbean.

INDEX

WHERE TO SHOP

◆◆◆◆◆◆◆◆◆◆◆◆◆◆◆◆◆◆◆◆◆◆◆◆◆◆◆◆

USA ONLINE

First World Imports – firstworldimports.com

Grace Foods – buygracefoods.com

Sam's Caribbean Online Store – sams247.com

West Indian Shop – westindianshop.com

UK ONLINE

Afro Caribbean Store – afrocaribbeanstore.co.uk

My Afro Foodstore – myafrofoodstore.com

The Asian Cookshop – theasiancookshop.co.uk

Avila UK – avilauk.com

Blue Mountain Peak – bluemountainpeak.com

Carib Gourmet – carib-gourmet.com

Caribbean Supermarket
caribbeansupermarket.co.uk

The Fish Society – thefishsociety.co.uk

Grace Foods UK/Caribbean Food Center
caribbeanfoodcenter.com

Tropical Sun Foods – tropicalsunfoods.com

Vincy Foods/Caribbean Trade UK Ltd
vincyfoods.co.uk

◆◆◆◆◆◆◆◆◆◆◆◆◆◆◆◆◆◆◆◆◆◆◆◆◆◆◆◆

Acknowledgments

I would like to thank you for buying this book and deciding to make some room for Creole food in your kitchen.

I would like to thank my agent, Elise Dillsworth, and my editor, Emily Preece-Morrison. Big shout-out to Rosie, Ellie, Clare, Wei, and the whole team that guided me through completing this dream of mine.

I would like to thank my family. My father – just mentioning your name or talking about you still brings me to tears. You always believed I'd write a book: you probably thought it would be Creole Caribbean literature, fiction, or poetry, as that's what you used to correct for me. I remember getting angry with you, since I thought your comments were too harsh. I wish you'd read over this book. I love you. Thank you for making me the cook I am today. My mother, who covers me with love and support – since my father died, she gives enough love for both. She is the strongest, most generous, sensitive, and loving parent one could wish for. She's an ace cook, too, and I respect her so much. My brother Sébastien and my sister Cindy. We are a clan; can't wait to cook (and argue like we always do) again in the kitchen.

I would like to thank Pierre Antoine, the love of my life.

I would like to thank my friends Audrey and Daniela, who are like sisters to me, and Samantha, Jessica, and Thaïna for testing the recipes one way or another. I'd like to thank Jenny, Sally, and my group of Frenchies for encouraging me. All the students I've taught over the past few years, who have made me a better cook, as well as the customers who have come to my supper club. And above all I'd like to thank God, because my faith is also part of my culture and I believe He masters everything!

weldon**owen**

Published in North America by Weldon Owen, Inc. under license with Pavilion Books Company Ltd

www.weldonowen.com

Weldon Owen is a division of **BONNIER**

This edition printed in 2015

First published in the United Kingdom in 2015 by Pavilion

Text © Vanessa Bolosier, 2015
Design and layout © Pavilion Books Company Ltd, 2015
Photography © Pavilion Books Company Ltd, 2015, except those listed in Picture Credits

Library of Congress Cataloging-in-Publication data is available

ISBN 13: 978-1-68188-052-5
ISBN 10: 1-68188-052-0

Color reproduction by Mission Productions Ltd, Hong Kong
Printed and bound by 1010 Printing Internatrional Ltd, China

10 9 8 7 6 5 4 3 2 1

Picture Credits:
Photography by Clare Winfield except those credited below:
Pages 2, 10, 15, 21, 22, 27, 29, 30, 38, 64, 128, 155, 174, 196, 204 © Guillaume Aricique at Happy Man Photography
Page 9 © Vanessa Bolosier
Page 19 © Jon Arnold Images Ltd / Alamy;
43 © raphael salzedo / Alamy; 53 © Danita Delimont / Alamy;
117 © Chris A Crumley / Alamy; 150 © Hemis / Alamy
Page 13 © Mike Kowalski/Illustration Works/Corbis